Spiritually Single

Spiritually Single

Marcia Mitchell

BETHANY HOUSE PUBLISHERS

MINNEAPOLIS, MINNESOTA 55438
A Division of Bethany Fellowship, Inc.

Published by Bethany House Publishers
A Division of Bethany Fellowship, Inc.
6820 Auto Club Road, Minneapolis, MN 55438

Printed in the United States of America

Library of Congress Cataloging in Publication Data

Mitchell, Marcia L., 1942-
   Spiritually single.

    1. Wives—Religious life. 2. Wives—Prayer books and devotions—English. 3. Non church-affiliated people.
I. Title.
BV4527.M545 1984   248.8'435   83-15754
ISBN 0-87123-591-9

Dedication

To my dear friends,
Brenda and Fern,
Whose prayers continually
sustain me.

MARCIA L. MITCHELL is a free-lance writer from Washington State who is active as a seminar leader at writers' conferences. Besides her long list of published articles, she is the author of *Jenny*, a Heartsong Book published by Bethany House Publishers.

A former Bible Study Fellowship discussion leader, she enjoys teaching adult Bible classes. She also serves on the Advisory Board for Wycliffe Bible Translators and is active in her local church. She is a pilot and shares her husband's interest in western art, Indian artifacts, and antiques. They have two daughters.

Table of Contents

Escaping evil—don't wait
Where to go for help
Don't miss the small changes
The place of praise

Introduction

The basis of this book is Paul's message for Christians married to unbelievers: "The unbelieving husband is sanctified by the wife, and the unbelieving wife is sanctified by the husband..." (1 Cor. 7:14). What does this mean in practical terms—in everyday life—for those who are spiritually single? These devotional thoughts and spiritual insights may help you to understand and apply in very specific ways the awesome-sounding word "sanctified."

Here are some suggestions for using the material in this book:

1. *As a once-a-week personal devotional reading for four months.* The weekly format helps to prevent "breezing through" some rather weighty issues without personal application. Time should be given to working through the study questions and making changes as needed in one's life.

2. *As a study project with a prayer partner or close friend.* A strong, open relationship with another Christian may provide a good atmosphere for using the book together. This joint study would create an effective springboard for constructive action; shared burdens seem less overwhelming and solutions are then more tangible and workable.

3. *As a textbook workbook for group study.* In such a setting, the members of the group should have a strong commitment to each other and feel free to bare their per-

11

sonal lives without fear that their privacy will be compromised. A group with common concern for spiritual singleness could find immense support and further insights beyond the confines of these pages as they work through the book together.

4. *As a reference book for particular problems and questions.* Certain chapters may give help at a critical time in the life of one who is spiritually single. The Table of Contents will direct the reader to the section which would be most helpful. Pastors and Christian counselors will find the book helpful when using it in this manner.

Our main concern is that you *use* it. Because the insights in this book come to you from the heart of one who has traversed a similar dark tunnel, they have been proven. Use them as candles to light your way, to keep yourself from losing your way in the confusion that sometimes comes. You will grow. You will become strong. You will triumph.

Chapter 1: *Promises, Promises, Promises*

"Remember thy word unto thy servant, upon which thou hast caused me to hope" (Ps. 119:49, KJV).

Writing this book, like getting my pilot's license, has been one of the most difficult things I've ever done. As a person who loves a challenge, I love life. I want to enjoy every moment of it. But I also want things to be done "right." And, in one area of my life, something wasn't right.

Shortly after our wedding I discovered that my husband and I held completely different viewpoints on the role that religion and church was to play in our lives. I was used to going to church every time the doors were open. If I wasn't busy every moment of the day "doing something for God," then I wasn't being a *good* Christian.

At first my husband tolerated my religious schedule. But, as the years slipped by and he watched the physical and emotional drain on me as I spent time, energy and money on the church—when he thought I should be at home— then resentment set in. Any *good* I was doing for "others" was paralleled by the negative reaction of my husband. It was a whirlpool that dragged me constantly away from him and, unfortunately, I was blithely unaware that I was caught. I thought I was swimming, and . . . "doing quite well, thank you." Instead I was being sucked farther and farther away from him until our worlds rarely touched and I wondered at times why we even stayed married.

I tried everything I could think of to get my husband saved. "If only he'd become a Christian," I reasoned, "then we could do twice as much for God." Then I'd feel guilty that only one of us was working for God and I'd try to do more to make up for what my husband wasn't doing.

As time slipped by and there was no change in him, I began to feel the loneliness and yes . . . the shame . . . of being married to a non-Christian. Oh, I'd smile as I sat in church and tell people I was "just fine," but inside I was crying— and no one seemed to understand.

There were times when it was acutely painful living a single Christian life—like when the doctor said I needed surgery and I couldn't go home and say, "Honey, pray with me." Other times, when I'd be reading a passage of scripture and some special truth would leap right off the page, without thinking, I'd turn to share it with him, only to be met by a frown, and the joy died on my lips, untold. I was married, but when it came to spiritual things, I was definitely single.

Throughout our years of marriage I've made innumerable mistakes, learned many lessons, and matured spiritually. At first I thought I was alone with this dilemma, but I've learned that I have unknown numbers of spiritually single sisters who are facing these same problems, experiencing these same emotions . . . and yes, making the same mistakes.

Now, after more than twenty years of marriage, hundreds of discussions over countless cups of tea, I've attempted to put some of what I've learned on paper. Other women, just like me . . . and possibly you . . . have gleaned some vital truths that have given us a better perspective on our lives.

To be sure that we are speaking the same language, let me define what I mean by a Christian. In this book when I say a person is a Christian I mean this: someone who has specifically confessed their sins to God, asking His forgiveness, and in return accepted the atonement of the blood of Jesus Christ. Only a Christian can claim that Jesus died in their place.

The Scripture tells us: "For if you tell others with your own mouth that Jesus Christ is your Lord, and believe in your own heart that God has raised him from the dead, you will be saved. For it is by believing in his heart that a man becomes right with God; and with his mouth he tells others of his faith, confirming his salvation" (Rom. 10:9, 10, TLB).

Just because a person says he is a Christian doesn't mean that he really is one. Throughout this book when I mention being a non-Christian, an unbeliever or unsaved person, I am referring to someone who has *not* made this very personal commitment to Christ.

In these next chapters we'll be looking at some personal situations in the lives of other Christian women. Biblical characters as well as contemporary women are our sisters in more ways than just by our faith. They've shared the same dilemmas, the same heartaches and struggles. But there is joy, too, as they have sought and learned the precious truths of God's greatness.

Perhaps the most valuable thing we can learn is how to apply those truths in our own lives. God wants us to live victoriously and yet we often settle for far less when we don't have to. It's been estimated that there are up to 30,000 promises in the Bible. In all honesty, can you say you've actually claimed even one of those promises today? Look at the immeasurable hope God is offering each of us personally. With a bit of concentration we can learn to appropriate many of these promises into our daily lives.

Just for a moment try to imagine with me the drastic change in your own life if you really believed every one of those 30,000 promises. As a writer I love to play the "What If" game. So in this case let's play it together. What if you believed, I mean really believed, even half of all those promises. That's FIFTEEN THOUSAND promises!

What if we, as Christian women, wives and mothers claimed just *one* of those promises every day for a year. That's 365 promises, only about 1% of the promises available. Do you know the change it could make? Not only would your life be changed personally, as well as your attitudes and actions, but the other people around you would change, too. Your husband, your children and even your neighbors and co-workers would change.

What if, for example, you really believed the promise that "all things work together for good to them that love God, to them who are the called according to his purpose" (Rom. 8:28, KJV)? Now really project yourself into the changes this one promise could make in your life.

If this promise is true, then being married to your husband, your *unsaved* husband, is going to work in conjunction with other things for *good*. If it's going to work out for good, and God has promised that it will, would you be as uptight or as critical in your daily life as you perhaps are?

The key word here is "all." God doesn't give us just part of a promise. There's nothing half-hearted in it. God is saying to us that every aspect of our life, every frustrating, panic-filled moment of it is meant to work together for good. That's almost unbelievable. I have whole days that seem totally lost as far as *good* is concerned. Events and circumstances toboggan from gray to ink-black in record time and I can't see any good in it anywhere. Yet God has promised. Dare I call Him a liar?

How much more relaxed I would become if I really believed just this one promise and lived by it daily. With this promise before me I can feel the tension and strain melt and drain, leaving me free to concentrate on the more positive side of my life. I know my husband would much prefer coming home to a happier, more relaxed wife; and who knows the good this one change might produce. I have to try; I owe it to him and to myself!

At the end of each chapter you will find some questions. Please don't skip this portion of the book. It's one thing to just read about possible solutions, but probably reading alone won't help you make the changes you need. Taking the time to look up the scripture verses and writing your thoughts will help you to retain the promises and apply the truths to your own life. All of us need to pause now and then and take a close look at our situation. As the promises and solutions come into focus and blend together, allow them to fill your life and create the changes that will bring the victorious life Christ has promised.

Promises to claim:
"For by these He has granted to us His precious and magnificent promises, in order that by them you might become partakers of the divine nature" (2 Pet. 1:4).

"Now the God of hope fill you with all joy and peace in believing, that ye may abound in hope, through the power of the Holy Ghost" (Rom. 15:13, KJV).

Chapter 2: *Created for a Purpose*

"This is now bone of my bones, and flesh of my flesh; she shall be called Woman, because she was taken out of Man" (Gen. 2:23).

"For this cause a man shall leave his father and his mother, and shall cleave to his wife." The minister stood three paces in front of us and a tingle rippled up the back of my neck. "And they shall become one flesh." He finished our wedding ceremony by quoting Gen. 2:24.

The stars in my eyes matched the skyrockets in my heart. I was young . . . in love . . . and now married to the most wonderful man in the entire world. In those first enthralling moments with "I do" still echoing in my ears, I silently vowed to make my husband happy.

In my naiveté I honestly meant it. After all, I loved him, and when you love someone you want them to be happy. But as days melted into years, my promise faded along with the naiveté, and somewhere I ceased trying to meet his needs.

As the awareness of our religious differences grew, I began quietly to put my own goals ahead of his. What began small grew into many conflicts of interests. In the process I wondered why our marriage wasn't everything the poets promised.

An early pitfall kept me mired down for a long time.

"How did I get myself into this mess, anyway?" The reasons that came to mind could fill a book all by themselves. In fact, when other women are discussing their stories with me I have a tendency to mentally say, "Oh, she's using reason number five or reason number three." I don't mean to be facetious, but we all seem to blame our circumstances on similar things. It's a bog that can keep you so firmly entrenched that you'll never be able to move onward in the healing process. The simple truth is, at this point, it doesn't matter *how* you ended up in an unequally yoked marriage. You can't go back and change it (no amount of lamenting it will help). Therefore, you need to face it as a fact—it exists.

Once you have given up your lamentation, the next question is, "Where do I go from here?" I found that the best place to go was back to God's creation of man and woman. We need to know where we came *from* in order to know where we are *going* and how to *get* there. The key to understanding my problem came when I reaffirmed that God created man first and then created woman. It wasn't easy for me, but it was right.

Being the only girl in a large family of boys, I remember always pushing to do everything they could do. Somewhere inside me there still remains a burning challenge to compete, not only with my brothers, but with all men. In order to survive, I felt that I *must win*. Although this is a common feeling among many women, its commonness does not mean it is God's way. It did nothing to make for peace in my home. It did cause me to search for an answer, though.

The second chapter of Genesis provided the answer to my underlying question, "Who am I?" When we know *who* we are, we can quit wasting energy searching from place to place. Instead, we can concentrate on becoming the best "ME," and it's all possible with God's help.

"And the Lord God said, 'It isn't good for man to be alone; I will make a companion for him, a helper suited to his needs' " (Gen. 2:18, TLB). That was when He made all the animals, but nothing filled man's needs. So God created the most unique being of all. God saw a need and created a being to meet it—YOU! There it is; woman was created to meet a *need*. We—you and I—have been created by God for a purpose.

How special that makes me feel. God created me with a divine purpose in mind. My entire person—my body, my spirit, my emotions, my mind—was specifically planned and formed by God for His use.

God knew what kind of man I needed—one who was strong and as steady as Mt. Rainier. But my husband wasn't created for me—*I* was created *for him*.

Please don't toss aside the book at this point, especially if you are a strong-minded woman. Although I *do* advocate putting things in their proper order, it will take great strength of character to follow the suggestions in the next chapters. In no way will it diminish your womanhood; rather, it will enhance you.

Getting things into proper perspective . . . just exactly *why* were we created in the first place? Scripture says: (1) to be a helper to man and, (2) to be suited to man's needs (Gen. 2:18, 20). This means you are your husband's helper, not his leader.

I can hear the groans all the way from your house to mine. You are saying, "But my husband will lead us the wrong way" or "He isn't the strong type so I have to be the leader." Then here comes your first challenge. Help him to discern his proper role as head of the household; help him find the path he should take.

Maybe you have a strong husband, like mine, and like me, you think you know "best" or at least you want equal time. Look at it this way. What if one of the disciples—Peter for example—suddenly decided to take over. "It's time for some equal opportunity," he says. "So, Jesus, you step down and let *me* lead for a while. I've got some good ideas and I think they're better than the ones you've been using."

I can hear your gasps! Of course it would be sacrilegious to usurp the position of Christ. The same thing is true in a marriage. Since marriage is a prototype of our relationship to God (Eph. 5), how could we dare to step outside God's plan for us? I'd much rather be the bride than the bridegroom. This means that by divine design and choice, I have a special role to fill—a role of equal value in God's sight, but of a different function.

Although the foot and the hand both have five digits, the foot just can't function in place of the hand. In some cases, when a hand is missing, people try to substitute a foot, but it wasn't designed to work that way. At best, it's just a makeshift replacement.

So when a woman must fill the role as head of the household, at best it's only a substitute. She wasn't designed or created for that function. On the other hand, knowing what we were created *for* allows us to relax and enjoy our position.

As man's helper we enjoy the freedom from the responsibilities that a leader must bear. We enjoy the protection that our mate provides. He is our natural barrier from the stresses and strains of the world.

If we are to be suited to his needs, it seems to me that we must be there when he needs us. We need to be supportive of what he does (unless it constitutes sin). We aren't to "run down" his pet projects just because they aren't church oriented or something we like to do.

"But I don't like what he does," Sue protested. "Fishing is his life; he lives for those weekends. But it's so cold and wet and the fish are smelly and slimy! I hate it!"

Sue's reaction to her husband's hobby was a normal one. We talked about what she could do to fill her proper role, and both of us decided that staying home while he went fishing wasn't the answer. She then tried (and I give her credit for this effort) to learn to fish with him, but it was more than she could do to touch the worms or pull a hook out of a fish's mouth.

Finally we decided to focus on a supportive role. She bought a camping cookbook and started trying to make a fun situation of their meal times. It wasn't long before her husband joined in the efforts and now they plan together to make his fishing trips into a more rounded family outing. The reality of her change in attitude and efforts became evident at a dinner party. As all the men were talking about fishing, Sue began to brag about her husband's latest catch.

"But you should have tasted that trout after Sue cooked it," her husband beamed. "That sauce she fixed was great!" The happiness on his face was payment in full for all Sue's efforts. And, she learned a special truth: happiness in marriage is a by-product, not an end in itself.

Being supportive doesn't mean being stomped on or lowering yourself to a demeaning position. Rather, each person can shine in his own role, enhancing one another. You can make or break your husband by your attitude.

"She never wants to do anything I want to do" is a common complaint in a troubled marriage heading for disaster. You, as a supportive wife, have the ability to change that situation by your actions. Take a hard look at your marriage. Think about your husband as he was when you married him and then ask yourself, "Have I forced him toward what he is today?"

There's something else you should consider in being the person to fill your husband's needs. Your husband needs you to be all you can be as a Christian wife. It is God's plan that he sees the life of Jesus in you daily. You are God's chosen creation for this specific purpose. Remember, the role you have now is more important than how you became unequally yoked.

Chosen by God, you are created by Him for this unique position in life. Can you possibly put more importance on anything else? Do you dare place something else above God's decree?

Perhaps Rebekah offers us a simple example to follow. In Genesis 24, we find this lovely woman who is about to meet her husband for the first time. If you read her story carefully, you'll see that she was handpicked by God to be *the* helpmate for Isaac.

"Then Isaac brought her into his mother Sarah's tent, and he took Rebekah, and she became his wife; and he loved her; thus Isaac was comforted after his mother's death" (Gen. 24:67). The first thing Rebekah did was to meet her husband's need. She comforted him. What a fantastic way to start a relationship! What a fantastic way to continue that relationship!

1. By putting things back into perspective, are you showing your husband the love he needs and properly filling your God-created role?
2. If Jesus stood in your shoes, married to your husband, living in your circumstances, what would His attitude be?
3. By diligently searching through the Scriptures, comparing God's plan for the Church as His bride, what verses offer the example for you to follow as a wife?
4. In what specific situation in your marriage is God showing you a new attitude to adopt?
5. What, exactly, do you plan to change today in order to conform to God's chosen plan for you?
6. Promise to claim:
   "And God saw all that He had made, and behold, it was very good" (Gen. 1:31).

Chapter 3: *Stand with Dignity*

"I do not ask Thee to take them out of the world, but to keep them from the evil one" (John 17:15).

"Saturday is my wedding anniversary," Judy said, "and for 24 years I've prayed that my husband would become a believer in Christ. I've pictured that long-hoped-for day a million times. He'll come to me and say, 'Honey, I've given my life to Christ.' Then we'll live happily ever after."

Although I, too, share that same dream with Judy, I've also faced another truth. In reality there is no "happily ever after," even when a husband becomes a Christian. There will always be problems in marriage. The Apostle Paul spoke to those considering marriage, "Such will have trouble in this life" (1 Cor. 7:28). The truth is that all married people have difficulties.

The difference for Judy, and for thousands of spiritual sisters around the world, is that when trouble comes we can't ask our husbands to pray with us. Because they don't share our faith, there is a distinct spiritual barrier between them and us.

Our points of view differ in nearly every area of life. "How can I raise my children to believe in a personal God when their father doesn't believe?" "Should church activities interfere with family recreation plans?" "Shall I go to his office party on New Year's Eve or go to church for

24

Communion?" These are typical questions daily facing the woman married to an unbeliever.

There are unique pressures that we who are spiritually single must endure that others usually don't understand. We must live a circumspect life while walking a tight wire between two completely opposite lifestyles. And, ironically, there are people on both sides who are watching intently to see if we fall. Some of our Christian acquaintances cluck their tongues and say we are walking too close to "the world," while our non-Christian friends watch for inconsistencies between our testimony and our everyday life.

The secret to endurance is personal spiritual survival. We must constantly guard against the pull of the world and yet not let the peer pressure of some misguided, but well-intentioned, Christians destroy our marriage.

Linda told me that her Christian mother was constantly nagging her to attend more of their church activities. A typical phone call would end, "Well, if Bob won't go with you, just leave him home and go anyway. You should have listened to me in the first place and never married Bob. If you aren't careful, he'll drag you down with him."

Linda was frustrated, torn between wanting to please her mother and her church friends and the reality of being married to an unbeliever. Her mother, who could have been a spiritual pillar of strength, was instead, though unintentionally, providing the opposite, undermining effect.

The stress of trying to live effectively in both the Christian sphere and the secular world can sometimes tear us apart. It isn't my intention to try to judge anyone's actions with this book. Rather, I'll try to relate some insights that I've gained from my personal experience and from others who have also been married to unbelievers.

The woman who is unequally yoked may oftentimes feel as if she is completely alone. In her struggle to maintain a sincere Christian walk she needs to know that none of us is alone. In both the Old and New Testament we have the promise of His personal help. "I will never leave thee, nor forsake thee" (Heb. 13:5, KJV). Also, God has provided scriptural guidance and Christian friends to help us in our spiritual growth. There is no need to feel either alone or ashamed. With God's help we *can* walk that fine line between both worlds and hold our head up with dignity.

I think holidays are perhaps the most trying times for the woman who has to make a choice. Because of a conflict in lifestyles, she would rather go to church parties while "his" parties may include activities that are contrary to our expected Christian behavior.

Because she was taught to shun the appearance of evil (1 Thess. 5:22), Darlene always refused to go with her husband, Tom, to the annual office party. Tom reacted to her refusal in bitterness. It became a divisive situation in her marriage, and Darlene was afraid that Tom was considering a divorce. In a moment of rare openness, Tom told her that he felt the reason she didn't go with him was that she was rejecting him. And, when all the other men showed up with their wives, it made Tom look like there was something wrong with him—a public embarrassment.

With a God-given sensitivity, Darlene now realized that this was a time when her husband actually needed her. She told Tom that she had thought he was trying to force her to compromise her Christian standards. Now, after 28 years of marriage, Darlene goes with her husband to his parties, being careful not to participate in the unchristian activities and yet being pleasant.

God seemed to honor her decision. At the very first party she met another Christian wife and they have become good friends. And, too, as she began to relax in her husband's circle, she allowed her natural fun-loving nature to show. It wasn't long before she became the life of the party, and others could clearly see that she had not compromised her Christian standards. This brought a renewal in her marriage with Tom.

In the book of Genesis we find an interesting example in the life of Sarah. She had a marriage that was far from perfect. Through the experiences of her marriage, Sarah had learned the balance between godly submission and refusing to compromise with God's standards. Though she was obedient, she didn't always keep quiet. For example, she demanded that Hagar and Ishmael be sent away after Isaac was born and God backed her up (Gen. 21:10-12). Yet, in 1 Pet. 3:6 we are reminded that Sarah obeyed Abraham and called him "lord" (Gen. 18:12). When we respect our husband's wishes, not as a doormat but graciously, we can enhance our marriage and display behavior that is precious in God's sight. And, it is through this behavior that God has promised to win some people to the Lord (1 Pet. 3:1).

There is a quiet dignity that comes with doing what is right. With careful prayer and searching, we can find exactly where that delicate line is and walk it gracefully.

1. What activity has your husband been asking you to participate in? (This could be bowling, football games, skiing, attending a local auction, etc.)
2. What do you think Christ's attitude would be concerning this situation?
3. Can you find a scripture verse that would offer the right example to follow?
4. How can you change your personal attitude to make it fit with Christ's example?
5. What action, if any, do you need to take?
6. Promise to claim:
   "But let it be the hidden person of the heart, with the imperishable quality of a gentle and quiet spirit, which is precious in the sight of God" (1 Pet. 3:4).

Chapter 4: *Bending the Twig*

"Train up a child in the way he should go, even when he is old he will not depart from it" (Prov. 22:6).

We have all been told, and rightly so, that the early training of our children is perhaps the most important time in their lives. But what is a Christian mother to do when her mate firmly states that he doesn't want all that "religious garbage" fed to his children?

When one of the dearest and strongest influences in the lives of your young children takes a firm stand contrary to basic Christian beliefs, your own personal involvement in their early training becomes imperative. If you are raising children in a spiritually divided home, your influence must be strong. When it comes to the spiritual training of your children, you cannot afford to be timid. As parents we are idolized by our children. They will follow in our footsteps far closer than we ever imagined.

Cathy knew the importance of prayer and spiritual training for her children. Yet, each time she tried to bring "religion" into her home, her husband, George, demanded that she stop. When she tried to have evening or bedtime prayers with them, George chose that time to interrupt, criticizing her or making fun of her beliefs in front of the children. He allowed no time at the table for a mealtime blessing and Sundays were a struggle. If she stayed home from church, she felt guilty; yet when she took the children in spite of his harassment, they all were usually in tears by the time they left. There seemed to be no right way to handle the situation.

The New Testament character Timothy was the product of a spiritually divided home. His father, a nonbelieving Greek, had some definite ideas on how his son should be raised. As the head of his household, this father was neither passive nor complacent. In contrast, Timothy's mother, Eunice, as a Jewess would have wanted her son to fully participate in all the traditions of her background. But one of the main ceremonies, circumcision, was denied to her son (Acts 16:3). The Jews and the Greeks differed greatly on this issue.

It seems that Timothy's father had the greater influence in this most important decision. Timothy was not allowed the privilege of this ceremony until he became a man and could choose for himself.

However, Timothy's mother certainly did not take a backseat when it came to influencing her son. Although she had to yield to her husband in some situations, she chose to do all she could in other areas, not allowing her sincere beliefs to be completely erased. In the quietness of her home, perhaps in the nursery, she used every possible opportunity to teach her son.

From childhood Timothy was taught to believe in God. In 2 Tim. 3:15 we read, "And that from childhood you have known the sacred writings which are able to give you the wisdom that leads to salvation through faith which is in Christ Jesus." Eunice did not wait until Timothy was a grown man to present her beliefs. Some people try to wait until their children are fully grown so they can "choose for themselves" what they want to believe. But waiting that long will be too late! "As the twig is bent, so grows the tree."

Our children are constantly being exposed to new ideas and influenced by everyone they meet. School, TV, advertising, magazines, movies, etc., all make a definite impression on their lives. We dare not be lax when it comes to the most important choice they will ever make. Christian training must begin in those early, formative years. Using the tools that are available, this very important training can begin today.

Eunice used the tools that were available to her. Probably the only written material would have been the Jewish Scriptures, our Old Testament. She made sure that Timothy truly understood the meaning of the Scriptures. To impart this much understanding would involve more than just reading a Bible story at bedtime or teaching a rote prayer like "Now I lay me down to sleep. . . ." Eunice had to put some time and effort into this early training.

To follow her example we would have to set aside specific times each day to spend alone with our children. We would need to clearly teach them God's truths through use of the Scripture and prayer. With the vast amount of Christian printed material available today, this task is much easier for us than for Timothy's mother.

To start your own creative ideas flowing, here are a few examples of things you can do to create a God-centered atmosphere for your children in your own home:

1. Use bright, colorful posters that emphasize biblical principles.
2. There are a vast amount of Bible games and activity books available. Use them to teach biblical principles and assist in memory work.
3. Memorize some portion of the scripture *with* your child each week. (Remember those promises I've been talking about?) Also, tuck a verse of scripture into your child's pocket or lunch sack each day.

4. Use books! Haunt your Christian bookstore and glean the best books available for your children. Read aloud Christian-oriented stories to young children and buy Christian adventure/romance for your reading-age children.

In order to combat any negative influences, we need to use every available opportunity to train our children. It wasn't the quantity but rather the quality of training Eunice provided that made the difference in Timothy's life. By making sure her son fully understood the meaning of the Scripture, she laid a solid foundation for his future. This knowledge gave him wisdom that later led to his salvation in Christ Jesus. It was Eunice's training that made possible Timothy's choice to believe in Christ.

But, as a mother, she received an even greater reward. Not only did her son become a believer, but through the further training provided by the Apostle Paul, Timothy became an evangelist. Because of a mother's faith, the early church received a beautiful spiritual leader and the world forever benefited by his training.

Cathy's situation certainly isn't unique, although every family doesn't necessarily face the same intensity of opposition. Raising just one child or a whole family isn't easy anytime, but when one parent is a nonbeliever, there are additional problems. She learned to be flexible in finding time to teach her children. She used short prayers throughout their day when her husband wasn't home. The after-school hours were used to offer a blessing over cookies and milk, prayer for help with homework or, for the younger children, a Bible story at naptime.

To cut down on the "Sunday Syndrome," she had a long talk with George and explained exactly how important basic religious training was to her. So they agreed that she could take the children to Sunday school. That meant she would be gone from their home only an hour and a half (including travel time). When George saw that it was only one and a half hours out of a week, he didn't feel so threatened.

In my own family I constantly had to guard against too much time spent at church and away from my husband. It was all too easy to add "just one more" activity for the children. Each family has to work out the balance that best suits them.

1. How can you lovingly ease the antagonism or threat that religion poses to your husband regarding your children?
2. What do you think Christ's attitude would be concerning this situation?
3. Can you find a scripture verse that would offer the right example to follow?
4. How can you change your personal attitude to make it fit with Christ's example?
5. If you have the responsibility of children or even grandchildren, what steps can you take today toward improving the quality of their spiritual training?
6. Promise to claim:
   "Believe on the Lord Jesus Christ, and thou shalt be saved, and thy house" (Acts 16:31, KJV).

Chapter 5: *You Aren't Single*

"Wives, fit in with your husband's plans. . . . Your godly lives will speak to them better than any words" (1 Pet. 3:1, TLB).

Knowing how to act in the sphere of your church is probably one of the more constant problems that you face. Week after week there are openings in areas of service that need people to fill them. Sunday school classes need teachers, boards need members, the office needs volunteers. The list is endless.

Exactly how much you are to be involved in these activities is a decision that must be made over and over again. Part of the problem is that others in the church see only *you*. If your husband doesn't attend church or many of its activities, you are always seen alone. I don't know why the single person is viewed as a prime target to do "just this one thing," but it's true.

Maybe it's psychological—if they don't *see* a husband, he isn't in the picture. It's assumed that you make all the decisions because you are the only one they see.

"Can you sing in the choir every night this week during our special services?" This question comes up twice a year in my church and I dread it every time. For the families who are church-oriented, a week's commitment is something special and together they can work their usual activities around that commitment. But for the spiritually single person it becomes a heavy burden. How do you tell your husband that you are going to be away from home every night? That means time away from him, an interruption of his plans, all for an activity that he views as unnecessary. When he sees the church and its program eating up your time and draining your energy, he will probably feel defensive and view it as subversive.

Yet, the people in most church circles don't understand that point of view. Rather, they telephone and say how much you are *needed* and plead for your help. The pressure from both sides often makes the wife feel as if she's caught in a vise. Sometimes she's made to feel like she isn't quite living up to her Christian commitment if she isn't constantly involved in church activities.

But you aren't single! You're married and your first consideration in these matters is to your husband. When there are extra meetings, you need to plan them ahead of time with your husband so he doesn't feel as though you are deserting him.

When you are asked to teach a Sunday school class or sing in the choir, remember to count the cost. It's so easy to fall into the trap of "doing your own thing" at church. There is a subtle sense of freedom to do all the "things you've wanted to do" when you are at church and your husband doesn't need to know. From 9:30 until noon on Sunday you can be "Mrs. Active Christian" and then keep quiet about it at home.

But singing in the choir usually means an evening of practice each week (with additional practices near the holidays); teaching involves study and preparation at home. How will your husband accept the amount of time and energy, or even financial expense, in these activities?

Perhaps the most important thing to remember in this aspect of your Christian walk is to maintain a proper balance. You should be able to work out with your husband the privilege of attending at least one church service each week. It isn't unreasonable in any marriage to spend one hour away from home for spiritual renewal. But you may have to make some sacrifices by choosing a worship service over other good Christian activities.

If there are children in your home, they need spiritual sustenance, too. You may have to elect to attend Sunday school with them, foregoing the main worship service. However, should your husband agree to your being gone an entire morning, then Sunday school and church are a double blessing.

The Bible does not say that you have to attend church *every* time the doors are open. We are told not to forsake "our own assembling together . . . but encouraging one another. . ." (Heb. 10:25). God understands your needs and situation. He is able to provide over and above what your church schedule may include. He is not limited to church meetings in defining what "assembling together" means.

The balance is achieved in what you *need* to sustain your spiritual life and what is extra or unnecessary. It's sometimes difficult to make this choice with so many well-intentioned people pressuring you. But when you see it through your husband's eyes, perhaps your time will fall into better perspective.

The same balance and knowledge that you aren't single applies to financial contributions, too. Sandy and Karen faced the problem of wanting to give money to the church.

Sandy watched the clerk add up her groceries, then quickly wrote out the check for five dollars more than the total. That would take care of the Thanksgiving offering. She pressed her lips together firmly, *And Larry will never know.*

I've done it before, she thought on the way home, *and he's never suspected.*

At home she quietly filled out the offering envelope and slipped it inside her Bible. *That's one place Larry never looks*, she thought smugly, *and, it will be handy for tomorrow's offering.* As usual she scanned the opened page. Any opportunity to read the Bible, no matter how short, was welcome. She'd opened randomly to the third chapter of 1 Corinthians and noticed the thirteenth verse was underlined. "Each man's work will become evident; for the day will show it, because it is to be revealed with fire; and the fire itself will test the quality of each man's work."

Fire reveals both good and bad, she thought, then paused. What would fire reveal about the quality of *this* gift? She picked up the envelope and its edges seemed to burn her fingers. "It would reveal dishonesty in my grocery budget," Sandy said to herself as she began her list, "which means I've lied to Larry about our food bill. And," her throat tightened, "I lied to him about how much money I give to the church when I know he will disapprove."

"Lord," she bowed her head, "forgive me. I want to be a part of helping others this Thanksgiving . . . but I want to do it honestly . . . as a Christian should." A tear trickled down her face as she opened the envelope and removed the five dollar bill.

She placed the money on the dining room table and stood up a little straighter. "Perhaps if I tell Larry about the offering and the good it will do, then he will be willing to share what we have. After all," she smiled, "he cares about people, too. This way our gift will be given together."

There wasn't any guarantee that Larry would agree with Sandy's desire to contribute the money to the church. Sandy had to trust God in that matter. Matt. 5:23, 24 says, "If therefore you are presenting your offering at the altar, and there remember that your brother has something against you, leave your offering there before the altar and go your way, first be reconciled to your brother, and then come and present your offering." She discovered that living in obedience to God was more important than what she felt she was offering to Him.

Karen's dilemma was handled differently. She was sitting in church listening to a special speaker. "Tithing is God's will. It is clearly shown in the Bible." The visiting speaker was trying to encourage the church members to give more generously. Guilt made Karen squirm.

The small donation her husband allowed her to give to her church each month could hardly pass for tithing—yet, what could she do? Shame burned her cheeks as she turned away from the offering plate, empty-handed. She loved God and her church, but in this she could not comply.

"Do I ask you to tithe on your neighbor's income?" an inner, familiar voice gently asked.

"No, of course not," she answered mentally, puzzled at the strange question.

"Neither do I ask you to tithe your husband's income. That responsibility is between him and Me. Rather, tithe on what is yours. There are other things than money."

What could God mean? As a wife, homemaker and mother, Karen earned no salary. All her time was taken up with her family . . . TIME . . . of course! Karen could certainly give God a portion of her time!

In the weeks that followed, Karen felt neither guilt nor shame when the offering plate was passed. Into it, for God's eyes alone, she placed her gifts of prayers for others, a visit to an invalid, a cake for a neighbor, and a phone call to someone who needed encouragement. Each one was a tithe of her time and her love. "It is acceptable according to what a man has, not according to what he does not have" (2 Cor. 8:12).

If you find yourself constantly pressured to be involved in church-related activities, perhaps you need to memorize some phrases to help you say *no*. For example, "I'd love to do that, but my time schedule just doesn't permit adding another responsibility." Or, "Thank you for asking. I'll check with my husband and see if it fits into our schedule." Remember what the Lord revealed to Karen: only God's approval of our lives is what is necessary for victory and joy.

1. What ways can you think of to make your husband more "visible" in your church life? (Include him in church social activities, invite other Christian couples to your home for dinner, talk about him as your unique helpmate, etc.)
2. What would Christ's attitude be regarding the balance between your church activities and your home life?
3. What scriptures would offer the right example for you to follow?
4. In trying to view your church life from your husband's point of view, what personal attitudes do you need to change in this situation?
5. What steps can you take beginning today to bring about a proper balance between your church activities and your home life?
6. Promise to claim:
   Wives are "to be sensible, pure, workers at home, kind, being subject to their own husbands, that the word of God may not be dishonored" (Tit. 2:5).

Chapter 6: *Preventing Spiritual Starvation*

"But grow in the grace and knowledge of our Lord and Savior Jesus Christ" (2 Pet. 3:18).

In the last chapter we said that you aren't single. Well, neither are you double. That is, if you are going to survive spiritually, you must do it alone. Your husband can't help you in your spiritual growth.

If you've had to trim your church time to the barest minimum, one thing you need to do is guard against spiritual starvation. This is the place in your life where you, and you alone, have to choose what your walk with God will be. The beautiful part of this choice is that God is so eager for you to choose Him that He has some fantastic blessings waiting for you. What you and I might see as a lonely, heavy burden, when turned over to Christ, becomes a gracious gift.

Remember Joseph in the Old Testament? Hated by his brothers, he was sold into slavery and left alone in Egypt. Yet, after his father's death, Joseph gathered those same brothers around him to comfort them. "And as for you," he said in Gen. 50:20, "you meant evil against me, but God meant it for good in order to bring about this present result, to preserve many people alive."

What at first had been a lonely, heavy burden for Joseph became a beautiful gift. Because of his suffering he was able to give life, not only to his beloved father, but to the brothers who had hated him, and to all Egypt as well. God really meant his trouble to turn into something good.

Joseph could have felt sorry for himself. And, quite possibly there were some dark times in his life when he asked, "Why me?" I know I have asked it more than once—especially when I'm feeling guilty because my husband doesn't share my faith.

Strangely enough, many of us in this situation needlessly bear a heaviness of false guilt. Put on our shoulders by other Christians, it's sometimes elusive to identify. When I first discovered that I was alone spiritually, I often asked my Christian friends to pray for me.

But as time—years—went by, and there was no change in my husband's spiritual condition, a subtle switch took place. My Christian friends began asking questions. "Are *you* being obedient? Are *you* being submissive? Maybe *you* need to change this area . . . or that one. Perhaps *you* are nagging him about God . . . or not saying enough." On and on the questions continued until I felt that somewhere I had failed.

If only I knew what the magic formula was, I could *do* it and miraculously the desired change in my husband would occur. But I never could find that formula. And I felt guilty! The truth is there is no magic formula.

I had felt there was something wrong with me because my husband had not changed. Because of this guilt I felt I was a definite failure and isolated from my Christian friends. When another woman's husband experienced a glorious conversion, I felt rejected and would cry out to God, "Why me? Why do *other* women get results and I don't? What's wrong with me?"

The reality and relief from this needless burden came when God showed me there was truly nothing I could *do* to cause my husband's salvation. I could change my attitudes and actions, but all I was doing was changing *me* not him.

Not that those changes were wrong; indeed, they made me a better wife, but *I* couldn't change *him*.

This didn't mean I was to give up and just say, "Nothing's ever going to change so I might as well do my own thing." I needed to go on changing. But the changes needed to be for the right reason to make a better person, a stronger Christian out of me, that God might be glorified. I would have to trust God with the responsibility of my husband's spiritual condition. I could pray for him and I could continue to change, making our home a more suitable atmosphere for God to work in my husband's life. But, I couldn't change him.

First Pet. 3:1, 2 says, "In the same way, you wives, be submissive to your own husbands so that even if any of them are disobedient to the word, they may be won without a word by the behavior of their wives, as they observe your chaste and respectful behavior." Whatever my husband's actions might be, I am not responsible for them. But I am responsible for my own actions and attitudes.

Margaret was feeling the pressure of inner conflict. When trouble came and her husband blamed their problems on Margaret's religious beliefs, she found a rebellious attitude was growing.

"I need help." Margaret sat in her best friend's kitchen waiting for a cup of coffee. "Bill is really pressuring me about my Christian life again. It just never stops. The minute we get one problem settled, another one or two take its place."

She murmured a thank you for the steaming cup placed in front of her and hurried on, pouring out her problems as the coffee was poured from the pot. Finally she slowed down. "I don't know what to do. Inside I feel so rebellious toward Bill . . . and yet, that isn't right. Lois, how can he see Christ in me with that kind of attitude between us?"

"Attitudes can be tricky things," Lois responded slowly. "I can't change the way you feel, nor can either of us change Bill's attitude. But we can pray together about both problems." She reached for her Bible. "This morning I was reading in the thirty-seventh chapter of Psalms. The fifth verse says, 'Commit thy way unto the Lord; trust also in him; and he shall bring it to pass' (KJV).

"Perhaps you're trying to bear the burden of Bill's pressure alone and it's affecting your attitude. Maybe you need to commit it to the Lord. He knows what is best and He alone has the power to handle it properly."

Margaret picked up the cup of coffee and took a deep drink. "I think you're right," she nodded. "I sure can't ask Bill to pray . . . but would you pray with me?"

The two women bowed their heads for prayer and Margaret sensed God's peace melting her rebellion away.

Margaret used a tool that is available to each of us in our spiritual growth. We are to "bear one another's burdens" (Gal. 6:2). Calling on a friend to help us pray is one of the best things we can do. Each of us needs a prayer partner, someone who can help us pray, but also give some guidance, too.

How often I've heard some well-meaning woman declare in a public service that her husband isn't a Christian and ask for prayer. Sometimes, in her emotion, she will include specific situations or problems they are currently going through that make me cringe inside. I've wondered just how her husband would feel if he knew she was sharing those details. And, it's very likely that he will find out.

How much better it would be if she had a prayer partner. Then, in private, she could pray more specifically and so could her partner. That would save a lot of embarrassment, not only for the husband, but for the people who don't know her very well and yet were forced to listen to her intimate problems.

In searching for the right prayer partner you'll need to look for certain qualities. She should first of all be a mature Christian rather than someone who is newly saved. Her spirit should be that of an encourager rather than critical. Sidestep someone who has a tendency to gossip. The things you'll share need to be kept in strictest confidence. In fact, my prayer partner and I have agreed that with certain subjects, "Unless it's *your* face in front of my nose, I'll say *nothing!*" You'll want a person who is well grounded in the Bible so that she'll point you to God for your answers rather than just dwelling on your problems.

I meet with my prayer partner at least once each week. But many times we'll use the telephone in between visits. So your partner should be someone fairly easy to contact. We always begin our prayer sessions with praise to place us in the proper frame of mind.

Be prepared for God to meet your needs. If you are this serious about seeking His guidance in your life, He has promised to answer. "And whatsoever ye shall ask in my name, that will I do, that the Father may be glorified in the Son. If ye shall ask any thing in my name, I will do it" (John 14:13, 14, KJV).

Many times in the privacy of prayer with a dear friend, God has spoken through her or in the calmness of His word, and I have found solutions that I wouldn't have heard in a large group. In these quiet moments it is the Spirit of God who teaches us. According to 1 Cor. 2:12-16, the Spirit of God combines spiritual thoughts with spiritual words and then teaches us what God wants us to know.

Progressing a step further inward in our spiritual survival, we come to the place of personal devotions. To prevent physical starvation we eat food every day. This is true, too, with our spiritual life. How many of us could survive on one meal a week? Why then do we think we can survive spiritually on one hour spent in worship on Sunday?

This is especially important to the woman who is married to an unbeliever. She needs daily spiritual sustenance. This can come only with a great deal of effort. Sometimes it takes a bit of creativity to provide the time for devotions.

Gloria kept a Bible in the bathroom where she wouldn't be disturbed. Donna used her coffee break at work for time alone with God. Joyce took the children to the park and read scripture while they played. The point is, we can't wait for that ideal time when the family situation allows for Bible study and prayer. We must actively create moments to devote to God.

At first this was difficult for me. But as I worked at it, my husband soon recognized this as my own special time. He would quietly leave the room, if he came in unexpectedly as I was having devotions, so I could have some privacy.

Of course, I'd rather have Bible study and prayer *with* my husband. But at this point it isn't possible. The Apostle Paul says, "I have learned to be content in whatever circumstances I am" (Phil. 4:11). The sooner each of us accepts the fact that this is our position in life NOW, the more quickly we can take positive steps in our own spiritual growth. We can't wait until "someday" to happen because "someday" may never come. We must choose to live and grow in Christ *now*, not later.

As you look at your very busy days, try to find a few moments to set aside for daily personal devotions. You may need to be creative, but then that's the joy of serving the Lord. He knows exactly the time spot in your day that is best for you. Ask God to make this time-space very clear.

1. In seeking to add spiritual food to your week, how can you inoffensively work around your husband's schedule? (Perhaps there is a Bible study group that won't interfere with your family situation. Maybe you could buy a Bible study book to use at your own convenience. Have

you looked into cassette tapes on good Christian teaching or looked into television schedules for possible Christian programming?)
2. What would Christ's attitude be regarding your devotion time?
3. What scriptures can *you* find that will offer the right example to follow?
4. What personal attitude should you adopt?
5. Who can you name that might be a suitable and willing prayer partner?
6. Promise to claim:
"But seek ye first the kingdom of God, and his righteousness; and all these things shall be added unto you" (Matt. 6:33, KJV).

Chapter 7: *Surviving Temptation*

"No temptation has overtaken you but such as is common to man; and God is faithful, who will not allow you to be tempted beyond what you are able; but with the temptation will provide the way of escape also, that you may be able to endure it" (1 Cor. 10:13).

It's lonely being spiritually single. In the crowd at church I've often ached for someone to fill that void beside me. We live in a couple's world. Tables are set for four; invitations state: Bring your spouse; classes are titled: Young Couples' . . . etc.

There is pressure to explain why I'm alone. It's one thing to say, "I'm not married," but a totally different picture when I must say, "My husband doesn't attend church or its functions with me."

People often murmur, "Oh, I'm *so* sorry," or make you feel like you've done something terribly wrong. It's like having a disease that has no cure. When a person is single, well-meaning people march right out and try to match them with another single person; but when you are married and still alone, they don't know what to do so they usually do nothing.

It's easy to withdraw from other Christians because of this social barrier. But if we do, our spiritual state suffers because we deny ourselves the nourishment of Christian fellowship. Consequently, we become more susceptible to temptation. There is a great temptation to say, "If only I had a Christian husband, then I'd feel accepted by my fellow Christians."

Connie was a young Christian wife who faced this pressure. And, as often happens, someone else saw her dilemma and responded. It began simply enough because they were both always alone at church functions. He would often fill that vacant fourth chair at a table, so they became good friends. Then they began sharing their problems of being alone in a non-Christian world.

A cup of coffee, lunch, automatically sitting together in church, soon became their normal relationship. Their hands touched as they shared a hymnal and a spark of emotion grew into a small flame. It wasn't long before Connie began to wonder if maybe she should leave her husband and marry a Christian. It just seemed that all her problems would then be solved. Life would be a blissful bubble of praying together, attending church together, reading the Scriptures together—absolute perfection.

With perfection as her goal, Connie began picking apart her own marriage. Small differences with her husband became large barriers. They quarrelled often and she determined more than ever to attain that blissful bubble of a Christian husband.

She was at a very vulnerable point in her life. I, too, felt that subtle pressure to conform in church circles by having a Christian mate. But one day, standing in a shopping mall feeling terribly alone, God provided an object lesson for me.

A freckle-faced little boy pressed his nose against the candy store window. His eyes, full of desire, never wavered from the delicious looking candy while his hands searched vainly through empty pockets. I was torn between wanting to give him the money he needed or the reality of frightening him, because I was a stranger. He finally pulled back from the window, sighed heavily and walked away.

I thought as he passed out of my range. *My nose is pressed against the invisible glass of God's law. If it weren't there, I might be tempted to reach in and take the "candy" that I had no right to touch.*

I stood there a little longer thinking about that invisible barrier. I knew I should be thankful for the security it provided. Because I'm a Christian, a wife and a mother, I want God's best more than I want to yield to temptation. And God teaches clearly that, if you're married, you must not yield to this temptation.

How often I'd longingly watched other couples who shared their Christian faith. They seemed so happy—at least most of the time. And when trouble came into their lives I was sure they knelt and prayed together.

Like the little boy, I sighed heavily inside and mentally pulled away from the tempting thoughts of a Christian husband. I shoved my hands back into my spiritually empty marriage and vowed to try harder. *Someday I'll be thankful for the invisible barrier of God's law that, like the glass on the candy store window, holds me back from yielding.*

One of the barriers God provides is Scripture. The Living Bible paraphrases Mal. 2:15 like this: "You were united to your wife by the Lord. In God's wise plan, when you married, the two of you became one person in his sight. And what does he want? Godly children from your union. Therefore guard your passions! Keep faith with the wife of your youth." It goes on in verse 16 to add, "For the Lord, the God of Israel, says he hates divorce and cruel men. Therefore control your passions—let there be no divorcing of your wives."

Guard your passions; control your passions—good rules to live by. But especially for the wife of an unbeliever, these words become a strong barrier to temptation.

It is difficult to control our emotions, but it can be done. One place to begin is in our thought life. Being conscious of what we are thinking and choosing to control our thoughts can stem the tide or direction of our emotions. Phil. 4:8 says, "Whatever is true, whatever is honorable, whatever is right, whatever is pure, whatever is lovely, whatever is of good repute, if there is any excellence and if anything worthy of praise, let your mind dwell on these things."

David, that beloved Old Testament character, had difficulty controlling his emotions and thought life. While his soldiers were out doing battle, David stayed home and took a midnight walk on his roof. In both of these instances he was in the wrong place at the wrong time. He should have been out with his soldiers, and if not with them, he should have been in bed at that late hour. Instead, he saw a woman bathing and yielded to the temptation into which the situation and his emotions propelled him (2 Sam. 11:1-4).

The consequences of his action were devastating! It drove him to commit premeditated murder, and the child of the unwarranted union died. David could have, indeed should have, returned to his own bed, controlling his emotions. Or, at the most, having desired a woman, he should have called for his *own wife*. He had a choice but chose the wrong action.

From the other point of view we have a more positive example in Joseph. A slave in the Egyptian household of Potiphar, he was constantly in the presence of Potiphar's wife. As can easily happen when two people are close together, Potiphar's wife finally voiced her desires aloud. Not only did she try to seduce Joseph once, but day after day she continually tried to get him into her bed.

But Joseph, caught in a circumstance where he could not physically remove himself, spoke plainly. Reminding her that he was her husband's trusted servant, he declared that it would be evil and a sin against God (Gen. 39:9).

It would be easy to look only at the negative results of Joseph's action. After all, it landed him in prison. But God, who promises to never leave us nor forsake us (Heb. 13:5), continued to bless Joseph even in jail. Not only that, being in jail was a step closer to the second highest position in all of Egypt (from God's point of view). And, that's where God wanted Joseph to be all along!

Like David and Joseph, Connie too had a choice. She could continue the relationship with her Christian friend, destroying her marriage, or she could choose a better path. When she faced the full reality of her situation, Connie chose to pull herself away—remove herself physically, until she could see more clearly and without the pressure of her emotions. When her friend called to meet her for lunch she turned him down; at church she deliberately chose to sit with other friends, making no room for him beside her.

As in the case of David and Bathsheba, Scripture provides an illustration that shows us what can happen if we make the wrong choice. Thus, by example, the Bible gives us yet another barrier to yielding to temptation. God offered David forgiveness for his choice but he still had to pay the price. Today we are offered God's forgiveness for our choices, too. Yet, as in David's case, there will always be a price to pay.

In the Epistle to the Galatians, the New Testament Christians received a precious admonition. "Brethren, even if a man is caught in any trespass, you who are spiritual, restore such a one in a spirit of gentleness; looking to yourselves, lest you too be tempted. Bear one another's burdens, and thus fulfill the law of Christ" (Gal. 6:1, 2).

This provides us with a couple of key thoughts. The first one is that *everyone* can be tempted. And the second key is that we are told to bear one another's burdens. When we are tempted it is good to remember that we are not the only person who ever faced this temptation and we need not bear this burden alone.

God has provided us with some barriers to help us make the right choices. First of all, the most natural barrier is our husband. Try, if at all possible, to place your husband between you and the temptation. Physically take him with you, linking your arm through his, to firmly establish the fact that "you are married!" Or, if he can't be there personally, then either stay away or try to never be alone with the "other person."

Believe me, God understands and He doesn't want us to yield to temptation. Even Christ had to face this same thing. "For we do not have a high priest who cannot sympathize with our weaknesses, but one who has been tempted in all things as we are, yet without sin" (Heb. 4:15).

God has given us Christian friends who will help lift our load. They can pray with us. Carefully chosen Christian friends will lovingly help restore us as the scripture in Galatians suggests. They, too, can become part of God's barrier shielding us physically and upholding us spiritually in our time of temptation.

If you find yourself thinking, like Connie, that it would be better to have a Christian husband, please think it through carefully. To defy God's clear command is a very dangerous position to be in. Remember that the consequences of sin is spiritual death (Rom. 6:23).

1. How can you use your husband as a barrier against any tempting situations?
2. What would Christ's attitude be?
3. What scripture offers the right example to follow?
4. What personal attitude should you adopt in your current situation?
5. Is there something you need to do *today* to remove yourself physically from temptation? (What close Christian friend or counselor can you seek out to help you bear this burden spiritually?)
6. Promise to claim:
   "For since He Himself was tempted in that which He has suffered, He is able to come to the aid of those who are tempted" (Heb. 2:18).

Chapter 8: *Love and the Broken Heart*

"I will . . . transform her Valley of Troubles into a Door of Hope" (Hos. 2:15, TLB).

When two people are married but discover they have completely separate goals or values in life, it can cause serious problems. This is especially prevalent in an unequally yoked partnership where the Christian partner tends to seek out other Christians as friends. These Christian friends can usually be depended on to help support each other socially, morally and spiritually.

But the nonbeliever more often will choose friends among other nonbelievers. This situation can cause quite a rift in the marriage since neither partner will feel completely comfortable with their mate's social circle.

Just as it was easy for Connie (in the previous chapter) to find someone who would fill the social void in her Christian circle, so the opposite can be true. The unbeliever, too, will have a void in his life that his wife probably doesn't fill.

In today's society, promiscuity is more openly accepted and current peer pressure makes it easy to justify by saying, "Everyone is doing it." But the Christian wife who discovers unfaithfulness in her husband finds herself in a very difficult position. How she reacts not only reflects on herself but on the body of Christ as well. People who know that she claims to be a Christian will be watching even more closely to see how a Christian handles the problem of unfaithfulness.

Janice was doing the laundry when she discovered lipstick—bright red—on her husband's shirt. It wasn't the first time. In fact, she had tried to ignore all the signs, such as coming home late from work and unexplained phone calls. There had been times when he didn't come home for a meal, and very definitely there had been a change, a distance, in their personal relationship. Now she'd found lipstick again, in a shade she didn't use.

Her dilemma was overwhelming and at first all she wanted to do was strike out in anger. Anger at her husband . . . how could he do this to her? And, anger at God, too . . . why would He allow this to happen? After all, Janice reasoned, she had been a loving, devoted, Christian wife. Why wouldn't God honor her stand and give her a solid marriage?

When there are serious problems between an unequally yoked husband and wife, it may take some drastic actions to bring about a change. For some people, the temptation to get a divorce automatically or at least become separated is very great. Life with the unsaved partner has been a tug-of-war, with each one trying to pull the family in his own direction, see-saw fashion. Now, with the problem of adultery added, it's getting worse. So it may seem like the only logical solution is to terminate the marriage.

However, as Christians we do have some sound advice in the New Testament. In 1 Cor. 7:10-16 Paul advises that if the partner is willing to remain with us, then we should keep the marriage together. Specifically verse 13 says, "And a woman who has an unbelieving husband, and he consents to live with her, let her not send her husband away." Nowhere does it state that there won't be problems in this kind of a union.

When problems do arise, too many times it's been easier to just call it quits and perhaps find someone else to marry.

"The *next* time," we tell ourselves, "I'll marry a Christian!" But another example, given to us by the Old Testament prophet Hosea, may help us find new strength to work through our problem *now*.

Hosea saw his wife, the mother of his three children, turning away from him to follow her old ways. She had been a prostitute and now she was rejecting him and seeking the pleasure of other men. The pain he felt and the depth of his love came through clearly in his actions. For her own protection, Hosea built a wall or a hedge around his wife. He didn't want her to go back to her sinful ways. He tried every way he knew to keep her safe.

In spite of all Hosea's trying, she left him anyway. But even then he continued to be aware of her. He didn't ignore her nor take another wife. He just couldn't seem to let go.

In the same way, Christ holds onto us. Wanting us to change, He pleads with us to turn willingly from our selfish ways. He stands with open arms . . . waiting . . . willing to forgive. "Behold, I stand at the door and knock; if anyone hears My voice and opens the door, I will come in to him, and will dine with him, and he with Me" (Rev. 3:20).

It runs against something inside us to forgive. Consequently, the ability to forgive has to be a gift from God. Christ became our example in forgiving when He cried out from the cross, "Father, forgive them; for they do not know what they are doing" (Luke 23:34). We are further admonished by Paul to follow Christ's example. "And so, as those who have been chosen of God, holy and beloved, put on a heart of compassion, kindness, humility, gentleness and patience; bearing with one another, and forgiving each other, whoever has a complaint against anyone; just as the Lord forgave you, so also should you" (Col. 3:12, 13).

What is there about a person who has yielded his life to Christ that allows him to forgive? It's because he's *been forgiven*! Knowing the balm and joy of forgiveness, how could that person turn away someone who is asking to be forgiven?

Yet, the next step is even more difficult—to forgive when the person doesn't *ask* to be forgiven. This type of forgiveness is completely beyond our human grasp. Again Christ set the example here, too. "But God demonstrates His own love toward us, in that while we were yet sinners, Christ died for us" (Rom. 5:8). We were undeserving of either His love or His forgiveness. His provision was made long before our desire for it.

In this step we can only claim the power of the Holy Spirit. " 'Not by might nor by power, but by my Spirit,' says the Lord of hosts" (Zech. 4:6). The Holy Spirit can work the impossible in us, causing us to love the unlovely and to forgive the deepest of hurts. Total reliance on His transforming power is essential.

Hosea's wife certainly did not deserve the compassion she was receiving from him. Yet, Hosea loved her anyway. The *things* she did were unlovable, but Hosea loved the person—his wife. God had given him the ability to see beyond her deeds and love the unlovable. It is possible to hate sin as God does and yet love the person as God does.

Hosea didn't give up. He didn't say, "Well, that's just the way it goes. She deserves the life she'll lead now. I'm glad to be rid of her." Instead, he remained active and began to woo his wife once again. Scripture uses the word "allure," carrying the meaning of enticing and persuasion. "Therefore, behold, I will allure her, bring her into the wilderness, and speak kindly to her" (Hos. 2:14). It took some careful planning and effort on Hosea's part to carry out this phase of his plan. He used *kind* words and took her to the wilderness.

Here, alone and away from the pressure of other people, husband and wife had a chance to renew their relationship. Each went into the wilderness with his own pain. There were no guarantees that solitude would work but the odds were in their favor.

In the silence of the valley, they could really listen to each other. They needed to be alone, just as we need to get alone with our husbands from time to time.

And, out of the quietness, the kindness and the tenderness, a new song was born in her heart. Heartbreak and heartache gave way to hope. There was a beautiful reunion, a new joy, a renewing of love between husband and wife.

God's commands to Hosea are very clear in the third chapter of that book. He said Hosea was to love her, try to win her back and to purify their relationship.

What was it that "the other woman" had to offer that caused Janice's husband to take the first steps away from her? Most of us would immediately answer, "Sex!" But there are actually many smaller steps that lead up to the final one.

Perhaps she was a good listener. There isn't a man alive who doesn't want someone to listen to him. All of us are flattered when someone shows an interest either in us personally or in the things we care about.

Maybe she was just "always there." Whenever he wanted to talk, whenever he had something to do, she probably was somehow involved. It's so easy to drift apart when interests or life patterns change.

My husband developed an interest in Western art. Since I knew nothing about the subject, it was easy to ignore this change. He began attending art shows, talking to artists and dealers and soon I was left far behind. When he'd ask, "What do you think of this patina?" and I only gave him a blank stare, it didn't help our relationship.

It quickly became apparent that if I wanted to continue to be a vital part of my husband's life, I'd have to do something. I began listening to him talk about paintings, and bronzes, asking questions, reading magazines and books.

There was a new sparkle in my husband's eye when I'd take part in a conversation with his art friends.

Over the years I've learned to share this part of his life. Now I go to the art shows with him and am as actively involved as he is. But it didn't happen overnight. I had to put forth some time and effort.

Like weeds, Janice began examining her own unwanted attitudes. There was initially anger. Then came jealousy, the bitterness of all her broken dreams, the pain of rejection—and much more. All these needed to be pulled from her life before she could move on to the healing process.

As Hosea must have done, she fell to her knees and earnestly sought God's help. Slowly, one by one the Holy Spirit dealt with her emotions, until finally, tears of submission to God streaming down her face, she yielded to His love.

"You loved me, God," she sobbed, "when I was unfaithful to You. Yet You forgave me. Give me the strength and courage to forgive my husband. Right now I don't feel very forgiving, but help me to become willing to forgive. Help me to lean on You rather than react to my own emotions."

Along with forgiveness, God showed Janice a key to weeding out her feelings of rejection. She discovered that she was relying more on her husband's love and faithfulness than upon God's. She found that God's love and the value He placed upon her life were a mighty fortress—an unshakable sense of true value despite what any person might say or do. This freed her to not depend on her husband for self-worth. She could now reach out to her husband in the security of God's love and acceptance. He might continue to reject her and despise her, but it would no longer rule her life.

Then, with God's help she began to try to restore the deteriorated relationship with her husband. She made a list of the areas of her husband's life that she did not share. There were some places he went that she decided it would be better if she made an effort to go with him rather than have him go alone.

Next, she took a close look in the mirror to see if she needed to make herself more appealing to him. Did she need a more updated hairstyle? Should she trim off a few pounds?

Finally, she began a painful examination of herself. Was she a good listener? Did she show an interest in her husband's activities? What about her own personality . . . was she fun to be with?

Janice knew that her husband's actions right now were unlovable, but then, hadn't God loved HER *before* she became a Christian when her own actions were unlovable? Diligently she sought God's help to see beyond her husband's actions and to love the person. It would take a lot of planning, a lot of effort, but she had to try.

If you are now living in this or a similar situation, you don't need to let it destroy you. Ask yourself what loving hedges or walls you can build that will protect your spouse, making him less vulnerable to outside pressures. If there are certain people or places that cause problems for your mate, try to find a way to help him avoid the situation. With prayer and God's help you can find the strength to try to restore your own relationship.

1. How can you show love to your husband in this situation?
2. What would Christ's attitude be?
3. What scripture offers the right example for you to follow?
4. Right now, what should your personal attitude be?
5. What *exactly* do you need to change in your life to create a better relationship between you and your husband?
6. Promise to claim:
   "But in all these things we overwhelmingly conquer through Him who loved us" (Rom. 8:37).

Chapter 9: *Don't Give Up Hope*

"Be strong, and let your heart take courage, all you who hope in the Lord" (Ps. 31:24).

Throughout the scope of this book we have focused on some of the main areas of stress that a spiritually single person experiences. Yet, there is another basic emotion that we all go through from time to time.

Discouragement can creep up and attack almost without warning. If we are aware of it, we can at least be partially prepared to handle an attack when it comes. It's not unusual to become discouraged when year after year passes and, in spite of all our efforts, there seems to be no change in sight.

Cindy, married for 35 years, shared her discouragement. "I have tried everything I know to do for 35 years," she sighed, "but nothing works. He's never going to become a Christian." She leaned back in her chair and pressed tense fingers to her temples. "I've tried to be the obedient wife, the submissive wife, kept my church activities to a minimum so they wouldn't interfere with his plans . . . but nothing happens! He's never going to change!"

Perhaps you haven't been married to an unbeliever for 35 years, but even a short span of time can produce some extreme moments of discouragement. The Scripture does not provide a magic formula, but it does give some powerful admonitions and promises to war against it.

Luke 11:5-13 talks about persistence. Verse eight says, ". . . because of his persistence he will get up and give him as much as he needs." It's the ask, seek, knock idea. Christ told His disciples to "ask and it shall be given to you; seek and you shall find; knock, and it shall be opened to you" (Matt. 7:7). Yet He stressed *continued* knocking.

We do not know *when* or *how* God will answer our prayers, but we are told to continue praying, persistently. Luke 18:1 says that "at all times they ought to pray and not lose heart."

No one ever promised that the Christian life would be easy. But God has given us so many promises to help, if we'll accept them. There will be times when we are misunderstood because of our faith in Christ. Mark 13:13 says, "You will be hated by all on account of My name, but it is the one who has endured to the end who will be saved." The reward for endurance is salvation, and that is certainly worth all the trials, testings and trouble that we face.

I think David caught my own feelings in the Psalms when he said, "I will try to walk a blameless path, but how I need your help, especially in my own home, where I long to act as I should" (Ps. 101:2, TLB). It's only with God's help that I can live the Christian life in my own home. If I persistently ask Him, God has promised to help me. "And whatever we ask we receive from Him, because we keep His commandments and do the things that are pleasing in His sight" (1 John 3:22).

It's so much easier for me to be "Mrs. Perfect Christian" when I'm away from home. But inside those four walls where I can't hide, my true self is fully exposed for my husband to see. I'm afraid the patience God asks us to display is one virtue I'm a bit short on. I don't like to wait for anything.

Yet, while we are patiently waiting for the salvation of

our loved one there are some positive things we can pray about. For example, we can ask God to create the kind of circumstances around our mate that will most likely produce results. Even as a farmer prays for sunshine and rain, so we need to include the right environment for our loved ones.

Additionally, in the Gospel of Matthew the Lord speaks of the harvest. He says, "The harvest is plentiful, but the workers are few. Therefore beseech the Lord of the harvest to send out workers into His harvest" (Matt. 9:37, 38). He doesn't say we are to pray for the harvest. The fields are already white unto harvest. But He does say we are to pray for workers. So, we can pray for God to send people into the lives of our loved ones.

With that in mind, Cindy began to pray for God to send someone who would be a worker for her husband. First, she prayed that God would lay a burden on someone's heart for him.

In a way, this changed the atmosphere in her home. She no longer felt the stress that she ought to be telling her husband about God. Cindy quit "preaching" at him. This allowed them to relax together without pressure. And, psychologically, she shifted the responsibility of her husband's salvation from her shoulders to God's. After all, God hadn't chosen her for this phase of work in the field. Paul emphasized this distinction: "I have planted, Apollos watered; but God gave the increase" (1 Cor. 3:6, KJV). She let go of the burden that God hadn't wanted her to bear. It was His job, not hers. Cindy's job was to pray for the worker, not do the work.

We can pray for that specific worker without knowing his or her name. Rather, we can pray for God to bless them and to provide the right circumstances and opportunities for them to work with our husbands. They will need wisdom and compassion, too. You can add to this list the specific things God brings to your mind. As Cindy prayed, it wasn't long until God in His own special way provided a knowledgeable Christian who was willing to share the Gospel with her husband.

With the assurance that we are asking because of the right motives and requesting the things God himself suggests, we then have the promise: "And this is the confidence which we have before Him, that, if we ask anything according to His will, He hears us. And if we know that He hears us in whatever we ask, we know that we have the requests which we have asked from Him" (1 John 5:14, 15). Aren't God's promises beautiful!

God doesn't lie! He has promised to honor our requests. But we can't stop just at the point of asking. We are told to have faith.

Faith is a unique word to explain. Perhaps the writer of Hebrews can help us understand it. "Faith is the substance of things hoped for, the evidence of things not seen" (Heb. 11:1, KJV). Substance is a reality, not a myth. It's something that can be seen. Someone once said that faith is a *verb*. If that's true, then our faith becomes the visible action of what we are hoping for.

Faith is Abraham striking out across a trackless desert in search of an uncharted promised land. Faith is Moses' mother putting her precious baby in a basket and placing it into the water. Faith is the priests placing their feet into the water of the Jordan river, expecting God to cause dry land to appear (Josh. 3:15). Faith is Rahab hanging a scarlet rope outside her window (Josh. 2:18). Faith is the children of Israel plodding silently day after day around the walled city of Jericho (Josh. 6). Faith is Paul and Silas singing in a blackened prison (Acts 16:25).

When Cindy saw how important faith was in her personal relationship with God she said, "Faith is like a spiritual thermometer. Once in a while we need to review our actions in relation to God's promises, like taking our spiritual temperature. Maybe I need to quit looking at the lack of results in my marriage and take a closer look at my faith in God's promises."

In other words, we are to act as though we already have the results of our prayers. The priests had to act as though the water had already parted. Moses' mother had to act as though she were placing that baby directly into the waiting arms of another woman.

Action is one of the more positive ways to defeat discouragement. Sitting around the house all day dwelling on your problems will make you a pretty dull person. If you have the spare time, why not learn something new—join a craft club, take an exercise class or learn a new skill. You're never too old to try something different.

I'm not a "hiking/granola bar girl," but recently I've started going for long walks during good weather or spending an hour at the gym club. Just a few years ago I learned how to fly an airplane. My family never knows what I'll tackle next but they've learned to expect the unexpected— and I think they secretly enjoy it! I know my husband likes to be around me when I'm doing something interesting.

I can't imagine Jesus just sitting around, tapping His fingers impatiently waiting for the Father to act. Scripture tells us that from the time Jesus was twelve years old, He was actively involved in *doing* His Father's business (Luke 2:49).

One of my main standby promises is found in 2 Pet. 3:9: "The Lord is not slow about His promise, as some count slowness, but is patient toward you, not wishing for any to perish but for all to come to repentance." When I begin to doubt and think that "nothing will ever happen," then I am reminded that all things come in God's time, not mine.

What *can* we do, then, while we are waiting God's timing? We can set aside our doubts, cultivate hope and maintain the action of our faith. But with these we can add the way of love. "But now abide faith, hope, love, these three; but the greatest of these is love" (1 Cor. 13:13).

The way of love puts our total life into perspective. There is the love of God toward us. "For God so loved the world, that he gave his only begotten Son, that whosoever believeth in him should not perish, but have everlasting life" (John 3:16, KJV). There is also our love toward Him: "Jesus said unto him, Thou shalt love the Lord thy God with all thy heart, and with all thy soul, and with all thy mind" (Matt. 22:37, KJV).

This love between God and man, properly channeled, becomes openly expressed to others. God commands us to "love one another, even as I have loved you, that you also love one another" (John 13:34). The thirteenth chapter of 1 Corinthians gives us a number of ways to express God's love: patience, kindness . . . "bears all things, believes all things, hopes all things, endures all things" (v. 7).

We need to spend some time loving the unbeliever "anyway." We may not love the life he leads or the things he does, but we are to love the person. Remember, God loved us in spite of all that we did before we accepted Him into our lives. Can we do any less?

1. How do you plan to change your prayers concerning your husband?
2. What would Christ's attitude be in your current situation?
3. If you have become discouraged waiting for God's timing, what promises can you list to give you new hope?
4. What personal attitude change do you need to make?
5. What new action do you need to take to help you feel better about yourself?
6. Promise to claim:
   "Let us hold fast to the confession of our hope without wavering, for He who promised is faithful" (Heb. 10:23).

Chapter 10: *With Love*

"An excellent wife, who can find? For her worth is far
above jewels" (Prov. 31:10).

As we ended the last chapter with the reminder that
whatever we do, we are to do it with love (1 Cor. 16:14), perhaps we need to examine more closely the "ways" of love.
The writer of Proverbs provided a beautiful description of
an excellent wife. By carefully examining verses 10-31 of
Proverbs 31, we can find new and better methods of fulfill-
ing our role as a Christian wife.

At first glance this woman sounds absolutely unbelievable. It would take an Amazon to perform adequately everything listed in these verses. This gal is a busy housewife
who gets up at the crack of dawn, makes sure everybody has
enough to eat and then heads for the market. There she
hunts for the very best of food, including imported specialties. She may relax a bit, keeping her hands busy sewing or
crocheting things that her family needs. In the meantime
she is checking over some property they need, buys it from
her own earnings, and supervises its development so they
can have a gain from it over the years to come.

After lunch this woman puts in a good exercise session,
checks to make sure everything is running right at home
and heads for a charity program. There she gets personally
involved, seeing that the needy are properly cared for.

Next, it's back to the business world where she provides excellent clothing for her family—things that create a good reputation for her husband. And, while she's at it, she creates a product that sells well to the public. This way she adds dollars to the family coffers.

Wherever she goes, she walks with dignity. You won't find this woman cringing in fear of the future. She takes it head-on, knowing she is doing her best to provide a solid foundation for her husband and family. But she doesn't keep all this effort and excellence to herself. Rather, in kindness she teaches wisely so that others may share in the knowledge God has given her. She doesn't have time for idleness or gossip. By suppertime she is back at home, overseeing all the work there, so that even in the night hours nothing is left unattended.

I'm sure she drops exhausted into bed and sleeps soundly before it all starts again the next day, just as the sun sends its fledgling rays into the crisp dawn.

When I first read these verses I couldn't believe that such a woman existed. I mean, doesn't she ever relax and do anything "just for fun"? But on a closer look (v. 13), the things she finds to *do* bring her happiness. And, there is a certain satisfaction in knowing that you do your work well. But perhaps the greatest joy a woman can know is shown in the last four verses.

Her children love her and show it. And what woman wouldn't love to hear her beloved husband telling her that she is the very best woman in the whole world? Even so, scripture doesn't stop there; it says even the public will praise her because of the work she does.

Verse 30 states the reason for it all. "A woman who fears the Lord, she shall be praised." I'd do anything for praise like that! Not that we condition our love to the praise we receive, but we all must admit that it does help stir us on. Love and praise from my children, along with the pride my husband has in me, would be fuel enough to keep me working hard for a long time. There it is, the full circle that creates the Amazon in Proverbs—work that produces praise; praise that produces energy to work again.

As women, we need to be busy; that's the way God made us. But it's important to control our busyness. *What* we are busy doing is very crucial. If we are busy in idleness, then all we are doing is spinning our wheels in place. We aren't going anywhere. It won't generate the praise from our children and husband. Therefore our energy is wasted and not renewed.

Betty is a bundle of busyness. She just can't sit still one minute. She plays the organ, sings in the choir, belongs to several women's clubs and is always taking a class in "something." Trying to reach her at home is an effort in futility. Many times her husband and children come home to find breakfast dishes still in the sink and a note saying, "TV dinners are in the freezer. I don't know what time I'll be home. Love, Mom."

"Love, Mom?" Where is the love in an absentee mother and wife? Oh, sure, once in a while we all get caught up in a situation that keeps us away from home. But in Betty's case, and for many like her, this is a normal way of life. They are so busy being busy that they neglect their first priority of being a wife and mother.

Prov. 31:30 reminds us: "But a woman who fears [reverences] the Lord, she shall be praised." If we want the praise that will keep us going, we need to begin by putting God first. With Him in first place we can then move on to our normal activities, knowing He will guide us in how we should spend our time.

For the woman who has an unsaved husband, how she spends her time is significant. If she is so busy running around "doing for others" that she neglects both her husband and her household, he will hold a very dim view of her

Christianity. He will see it only as something that separates them.

With that in mind we can now go back to the example of the excellent wife in Proverbs to find some loving ways to be the woman he needs. What are some of the things we can do to be a wife and mother like her? Perhaps we should start by dividing the day of the excellent woman and studying it. It breaks down into: food, family and fun.

If a man is hungry, then almost nothing else we do can really matter much. But the excellent wife not only provided food for her family, she found specialties, even imported foods (v. 14). My husband has a unique German-from-Russia background and he loves the food his grandmother used to make. If I really want to please him, I'll spend time baking crusty round loaves of rye bread and light-as-air Greble, a twisted doughnut-like dessert smothered in powdered sugar. These things don't come prepackaged at the supermarket. They take time and effort—but the praise he gives me is worth every ounce of energy I've expended. You can believe I'll do it again—and again.

The same thing is true with the family section. When my daughter proudly showed off her new dress at church and said, "My mom made this," I nearly burst my buttons under her praise. I don't sew for her as often as I should, but we've learned to turn a shopping trip into the same kind of specialness. It isn't the item that matters so much; rather it's the love behind it. "My mom did this for me" means the same whether it's the time you took to arrange your daughter's hair in a new style or the effort you made to find a special book on motorcycles for your son. The results are equal.

When your husband comes home to a clean house, contented children and a charming wife, you're nearly home-free in the game. And speaking of charm, a little fun adds a lot of charm to any woman's life.

Our "excellent woman" found something to do that delighted her (v. 13). When we are delighted there's a sparkle in our eyes, a glow on our cheeks and a smile on our face that adds immeasurable charm. It's important that each of us find something to do that delights us. As long as it's kept in proper proportion to the rest of our day, something "fun" puts a zest into life that adds considerably to our personality. But fun doesn't have to be ours alone. In fact, as wife and mother it's also our responsibility to see that the others in our family take time for fun, too.

How about planning some family activities that can be fun for everyone? Our whole family enjoys miniature golf. It gives us a chance to be silly together—and, when my husband gets into a go-cart he turns into a thirteen-year-old kid!

When was the last time you attended a local basketball (any sport) game with your family? For an evening at home there are literally hundreds of table games on the market that will fit every age group. As a nation we are saturated with recreational activities. It shouldn't be too difficult to find something that will fit your circumstances and tastes.

By closely comparing yourself to the woman in Proverbs, you may find a whole new lifestyle. Begin each day with a refreshing time of communion with God. Then in planning the rest of your day include something fun for yourself and for the members of your family. Change your day from one filled with busyness to something more productive. It isn't easy to break the mold of years of habit, but with God's help you can do it.

1. What special way can you show love to your husband today?
2. What would Christ's attitude be concerning your current daily schedule?
3. What scripture offers the right example to follow?

4. What new personal attitude should you adopt?
5. What specific action can you take beginning today to bring your life into a better balance? (What special thing can you add to your dinner tonight? What can you plan that will be fun for your family? etc.)
6. Promise to claim:
   "Since future victory is sure, be strong and steady, always abounding in the Lord's work, for you know that nothing you do for the Lord is ever wasted as it would be if there were no resurrection" (1 Cor. 15:58, TLB).

Chapter 11: *The Power Struggle*

"In the same way, you wives, be submissive to your own husbands so that even if any of them are disobedient to the word, they may be won without a word by the behavior of their wives, as they observe your chaste and respectful behavior" (1 Pet. 3:1, 2).

Submission! How I detested that word. And yet, there it was in black and white—in the holiest of books. I couldn't ignore it. Scripture says it more than once: wives be subject to your husbands. Why should I have to submit to him? After all, *I'm* the one who is on the *right* path. In this situation *he* ought to follow me!

In today's American society when women are choosing to step into responsible roles of leadership, both in business and at home, blind obedience is difficult to accept. But I don't think that God intended us to obey blindly. Perhaps a better way to view it would be "loving submission."

"Loving submission" means that the Christian wife recognizes her place as under her husband's direction (1 Cor. 11:3), whether he is a believer or not. She realizes that God is able to use and work through her husband to make proper decisions for the family. She will peaceably voice her ideas to her husband and then leave the decision to him. Right or wrong, she trusts that God will work through it.

Any time two people are competing for the leadership

role, it becomes a power struggle. And, in a power struggle there are no winners. Oh, one of them may end up "getting his own way" or dominating another person. But there are no real winners. The loser usually ends up submitting outwardly, while rebelling inwardly. That rebellion only sets the stage for the next power struggle.

As a Christian wife it's important not to be caught in a power struggle with your husband. If we know exactly what the outer limits are of God's guidance for being submissive to our husbands, then our actual areas of submission are clear. God is the one who set these limits. Then, by remaining inside these limits we are being obedient to God. This eliminates the problem of a power struggle with our husband and brings us freedom as we are in harmony with God.

Let's take a closer look at some of these outer limits. The most obvious one is that we are to obey God, not men (Acts 5:29). Another limit says we are not to yield our bodies to sin (Rom. 6:13).

With these two limits in mind we can rest assured that God does not expect us to obey our husbands if they are asking us to sin. It may sound ridiculous to think that any husband would ask his wife to sin, but there are some extreme cases that can't be ignored. Whenever we are asked to participate in breaking God's law, our obedience must skip over the head of the house and yield directly to God.

The only way to know what God's limits are is to study the Scriptures. Each person can then make his own list of do's and don'ts. For example, if your husband wanted you to help him commit murder, you automatically know that God forbids taking another life. But, as a Christian, what would you do if he asked you to sign a falsified joint Income Tax Return? God's law says we aren't to lie, yet how do you handle the problem of, "If my boss calls me for overtime work, tell him I'm not home"? The answers to these questions aren't as clear, and for some women who are married to non-Christians, these situations pose very real problems. In *every* situation there is a way out or a way through. "No temptation has overtaken you but such as is common to man; and God is faithful, who will not allow you to be tempted beyond what you are able, but with the temptation will provide the way of escape also, that you may be able to endure it" (1 Cor. 10:13). With prayer and diligent time spent in the Scriptures, God can provide each of us with a workable solution to our own unique problems.

Using those ideas as some outer limits, then how should we act in other, not-quite-so-heavy situations? Here our answer is very plain: SUBMIT!

Lonni wanted to attend an out-of-town religious meeting, but her husband said, "No, I don't want you to go." It was an important meeting in Lonni's life, one she had dreamed of, and now she finally had a chance to go. Except . . . her husband stood like a brick wall between her and happiness. Or so she thought. At first Lonni decided that she'd just go to the meeting anyway. After all, it's a free country, isn't it? But the problem with that was the feelings of guilt it generated—and the natural consequences of creating animosity between herself and her husband.

At last, after much prayer, she chose to talk to her husband to find out his real reason for not wanting her to go. She knew it wasn't financial and her family obligations were covered, so it had to be some deeper reason. Lovingly, without tears and heated emotions or accusations, Lonni began to question her husband. In the end she learned that he feared her involvement in what he called "the Church." Each new activity was viewed as a threat to his hold on her. In reality, he was afraid of losing her.

When she realized how her husband felt about this meeting, Lonni chose to stay at home. Not, however, with the "poor me" attitude, or a seething bitterness that her husband had "won." Rather, she chose to view this decision as a means of displaying her love. Of the two choices, the meeting suddenly lost its flavor. As a Christian wife it was more important to reassure her husband of his place in her life. In this situation obedience flowed from her loving submission and the power struggle was over.

Not every man would be able to state his reasons as clearly as Lonni's husband, even if he wanted to. In fact, he may be the kind of man who would not choose to state his reasons. In any case, as Christian wives we have the unique responsibility of looking beneath the surface of any confrontation. It's more important to meet the deeper needs and that's where we can allow Christ to help us.

Rom. 5:5 says, "The love of God has been poured out within our hearts through the Holy Spirit who was given to us." So with the gentle voice of the Holy Spirit speaking to our hearts, we can seek a better understanding of our mates. We can use that special sensitivity given to us by God to know when not to cross the line that would unnecessarily displease our husbands.

There are many important issues where we have to take a firm stand—like nurturing our children in the message of Christ or attending at least one meeting weekly with the body of believers. Why should we waste our "ammunition" on these smaller skirmishes? Wouldn't it be better to listen to the voice of God, appropriating His unique wisdom to handle these situations? (1 Cor. 2:12, 13).

Sometimes when we get our priorities turned around, we tend to follow our own emotions and feelings rather than to seek God's best solution. We are told by the Apostle Paul, "So then let us pursue the things which make for peace and the building up of one another" (Rom. 14:19).

Being a very headstrong person, I find it necessary to remind myself constantly that *I* am not in control. Again, Paul says, "But I want you to understand that Christ is the head of every man, and the man is the head of a woman, and God is the head of Christ" (1 Cor. 11:3). This is the way God wants it. It's only when my husband's decisions conflict with God's known law that I am to refuse to submit.

That doesn't mean that I am passive. In contrast to being a doormat I still speak up—maybe too often. But my husband wants to hear my point of view. It's *how* I express myself that is valuable. The Apostle Peter reminds us that our conversation is to be holy (2 Pet. 3:11). I'm learning to make a conscious effort to leave the final decisions with my husband—and ultimately with God.

1. If you find yourself in a power struggle with your husband, what can you do to show him God's love?
2. What would Christ's attitude be?
3. What scripture offers the right example to follow?
4. What changes should be made in your personal attitude?
5. What action, if any, do you need to take to stop a current power struggle and avoid future ones?
6. Promise to claim:
   "For the Holy Spirit will teach you in that very hour what you ought to say" (Luke 12:12).

Chapter 12: *The Art of Communication*

"Set a guard, O Lord, over my mouth; keep watch over the door of my lips" (Ps. 141:3).

"I've told Jim so many times that he ought to go to church with me." Teri nervously rearranged the cooky crumbs on her plate. "I can't count the number of times I've told him he needs to become a Christian. But he just won't listen to me."

Teri's husband Jim was an ordinary man. With no over-powering evil habits, I could picture his reaction to her preaching. He was a good husband and a good provider for the family . . . why should he change? In reality, he viewed her attitude toward him as unjust criticism.

Over the years Teri's religious nagging had become a strong point of contention. From the way he so quickly turned off everything Teri said, it was evident that she would never nag her husband into heaven.

Whether you verbally preach, or turn on a religious TV program when you know it irritates him, or even just leave church literature scattered around the house, it's still religious nagging. And, its only result is a negative attitude toward you—and toward God. Your husband will see you as only trying to flaunt a "holier-than-thou" attitude.

We have to be so careful when it comes to communicating. More than just words are heard. Our actions, tone of voice, attitude, even body language sometimes speak louder than the words we are saying.

Job's wife appeared to be like this. She seemed to be a nagger. Not only did she offer her husband no comfort or compassion, she blatantly told him what to do—and in no uncertain terms! "Then his wife said to him, 'Do you still hold fast your integrity? Curse God and die!' " (Job 2:9).

Poor Job—no one understood him, not even his wife. And yet we find some interesting hints on the art of communication in these passages. When his friends first came to see him, they realized that Job's situation was beyond words. "Then they sat down on the ground with him for seven days and seven nights with no one speaking a word to him, for they saw that his pain was very great" (Job 2:13).

They didn't have to say a single word, yet they communicated their message anyway. Some things are better demonstrated than spoken.

Love is like that. Although we need to hear words of love, too, yet those deepest emotions are better conveyed in actions. By our actions we not only show our personal love to our husbands, but also God's love. In Psalm 19 God provides a unique example of how to communicate an unspoken message. He describes the heavens, the stars and the sun. "Day and night they keep on telling about God. Without a sound or word, silent in the skies, their message reaches out to all the world" (Ps. 19:2-4, TLB).

We can follow God's example by knowing when to act quietly and methodically, permeating our sphere with love. Those around us won't need to be preached "at." Our unspoken demonstration, on a daily basis, speaks louder than any words (1 Pet. 3:1, 2).

Just as the scripture says there is a time to be silent, it also says there is "a time to speak up" (Eccles. 3:7, TLB). We aren't dumbwaiters, but we must know how to exercise both finesse and discernment. *When* and *how* to speak up are as important as *what* we say.

On a communicating level, *tell* him how much you love him. Openly say how much you need him and that you appreciate all he does for you. From time to time be specific. Include things like, "I appreciate how you faithfully work and financially support me." Or, "Sometimes I ache with loneliness; then you walk in the door and it all disappears." He may blush or shrug it off, but inwardly your husband will be pleased.

Another area of open communication relates to getting your husband's permission *before* you do something. Amy loaned some blankets and dishes to a visiting missionary. When her husband exploded, she countered with, "Well, we weren't using them. Why shouldn't I have loaned them?"

The problem was she hadn't stopped to figure out what her husband would want to do. If she had asked him, he probably would have gladly given his permission. But since she didn't ask, he felt slighted, as though his opinion was of no value.

Not every married couple would react the same way. In each marriage the requirements of communication are different. The more you melt together mentally, the less the emotional strain on the relationship.

When Amy realized that she had stepped outside of her authority, she apologized to her husband. And the next time a situation arose, she sought his permission first—*before* acting. Then, with his full backing she actually was freer to do more than she had done before—with no negative response from her husband. Instead, he was pleased to be included in her activities, as though the whole thing were his idea and she was just carrying it out.

On a more intimate level your husband needs to know he can trust you with his confidences. Whether it's valid or not, women have a reputation as gossips. One woman I know sometimes blurts out the most intimate things "so they can be prayed about." I know her husband would be embarrassed if he knew all she told and to whom she said it.

A man needs to have a confidant, someone he can trust with his innermost thoughts and problems. If a wife can be her husband's confidante, their relationship will deepen beyond belief.

But it takes work to create this kind of relationship. You may need to deliberately reaffirm that there are some things you just don't talk to *anyone* about. Or, you can say, "Do I have your permission to share this with a friend?" If he says no, then sweetly assure him that you will not betray his confidence. Trust is a thin line, whether it's strong as steel or frail as a cobweb. As wives, especially unequally yoked wives, we need to treat it with great respect.

Knowing *when* to talk with your husband is an art all by itself. I've learned to "read" my husband as soon as he walks through the door. If he's had a difficult day, I'll wait for a better time to discuss anything of significant importance or possible controversy.

On the other hand, when I've needed to talk to him about something important, I often spend time in prayer first. Then I've been amazed at how easily God fits the important things into our conversation in exactly the right atmosphere. I often need to be willing to wait for God's timing.

Being willing to wait for God is the secret to the success of a Christian wife. So many times I want to do things *my* way—speak up when I should be silent, preach instead of demonstrate. But God wants me to be yielded to Him in *all* things.

How quickly words spring from our mouths, sometimes with no forethought, and afterward we wish we could erase them. If only we would yield our motives and thought life to the purifying power of God, we would avoid some heartbreaking situations. But to willingly yield to Christ takes strength of character, control, and commitment.

It takes strength to clamp those teeth tightly shut when words would slip out too quickly. With constant control and an inner ear tuned to the whispers of the Holy Spirit, we can discern when to speak up and when to keep silent. But the greatest of these is to be fully committed to Christ.

The Apostle Paul spoke urgently to his friends in Rome begging them "to present your bodies, a living and holy sacrifice, acceptable to God, which is your spiritual service of worship" (Rom. 12:1).

That's what each of us needs to be willing to do. As an act of worship we need to present ourselves as a living sacrifice to God. But we must remember that this sacrifice includes yielding our mouths and words to His purifying power and control.

1. How can you begin today to practice the art of communication with your husband?
2. What would Christ's attitude be regarding your preachiness or nagging?
3. Which verses of scripture in this chapter have provided a new pattern for you to follow?
4. What new personal attitude can you adopt that will improve the communication level in your home?
5. What action, if any, do you need to take to get things moving in God's direction for an improved relationship with your husband?
6. Promise to claim:
   "May my spoken words and unspoken thoughts be pleasing even to you, O Lord my Rock and my Redeemer" (Ps. 19:14, TLB).

Chapter 13: *The Spirit of Joy*

"Walk in a manner worthy of the calling with which you have been called, with all humility and gentleness, with patience, showing forbearance to one another in love, being diligent to preserve the unity of the Spirit in the bond of peace" (Eph. 4:1-3).

"I'm a little bit frightened," Lara confessed to me one day. "What if my husband found someone more appealing to him than me?" She stared solemnly in the hall mirror. "How can I make myself more attractive?"

Her plaintive cry reminded me of two other women. It was at a Bible class and the discussion focused on what each person had done prior to coming to class. The first lady said she had spent the last hour making herself presentable. In her late forties, she had lovely salt and pepper hair. Her makeup was flawless and her clothes were stylish and immaculate. Anyone would enjoy being seen with her.

The second woman clasped her hands in joy. "I've just had the greatest time alone with God. The last hour and a half I've been reading my Bible and praying." There was an undeniable glow on her face. But the beauty stopped there. She'd made no attempt to "fix herself up" at all. Her hair was a bit tousled, her clothes rumpled and dowdy.

The two women seemed in absolute contrast to each other outwardly. Somehow there should have been a blending of them both. If the impeccably dressed woman had the added glow of the woman who had spent her time in prayer, she would have surpassed perfection. Contrarily, the second woman's outward appearance somewhat tainted the joy on her face. There needs to be a proper balance between our inner spiritual beauty and the time spent in making the outer person equally attractive.

No matter what a woman does, where she has been, or where she is going, a negative appearance or attitude, like a clashing perfume, will drive people away from her. No matter how "spiritual" she may be, the outer image a woman projects is the first and most lasting view of her seen by others. In fact, even after spending enough time together so that another person can discern the true spiritual depth of a woman, her "image" still is the most important in human relationships.

Queen Esther was a woman very much aware of the importance of her image. In her initial contact with the palace officials her personality made a favorable impression. "Now the young lady pleased him and found favor with him" (Esther 2:9). But she also knew that outward beauty was valuable, too. That same verse goes on to say, "So he quickly provided her with her cosmetics and food. . . ."

Esther knew that her appearance was paramount when she first saw the king. There would be no time for him to discern how knowledgeable she was or the depth of her spiritual life. She listened to the people in charge and took their advice. "And Esther found favor in the eyes of all who saw her" (Esther 2:15). Her wise conduct was rewarded because she found favor in the eyes of the king and he chose her to be his queen (Esther 2:17).

But she didn't stop making herself beautiful after she had won her man. Later, when her spiritual values were being severely tested, she did not neglect her outward appearance. Esther had fasted for three full days. Do you know what you would look like physically at that point? I'd look drawn and tired and weak.

Yet Esther chose to do this just prior to the most important audience she had ever requested. It was a time when she would be judged by her appearance. There wouldn't be time to explain to the king that she'd spent her last three days in prayer. So this time when her very life hung in the balance, she put on her royal robes. Enhanced by the inner glow of communion with God, she stepped out to meet her fate.

God honored her commitment. "And it happened when the king saw Esther the queen standing in the court, she obtained favor in his sight" (Esther 5:2). The king made his decision by sight—how she looked on that first impression.

If you were to move to a new town and drive around the streets looking for a new church, your first impression of that church would be its outward appearance. If the paint were peeling, the lawn overgrown and weedy, shutters hanging askew and litter piled against the building, you'd think, *Those people don't really care much.* I doubt if you'd bother to visit that church, even to give the people a chance to show you how "spiritual" they were.

The same thing is true with your personal temple. Scripture says that we are the temple of the living God (1 Cor. 3:16, 17). Haven't you ever heard someone say, "If that's what a Christian looks like, I don't want to be one"?

An overweight, ill-dressed, unclean, unkempt Christian doesn't do much for the positive advertising we need. In fact, it may so repulse the viewer that she may never have an opportunity to come into contact with the "inner person."

Let's face it. Christian or not, what husband wants to come home to a chaotic household, dirty kids, and a sloppy wife? (Her excuse? "I've spent all my time at church . . . reading the Bible . . . in prayer, etc., and didn't have time to do anything at home.") This kind of situation certainly won't help to create the best of Christian images. God is a God of order, not chaos. Think about the methodical way He created all things in Genesis, chapter one. Throughout the ages He has shown that He is a God of discipline and firm control.

God tells us that we are to be like Him. Therefore, when we show lack of control by gossiping, overeating, overspending, etc., we are not reflecting His attributes. Neither does lack of discipline shown by laziness, sloppiness or uncleanliness reflect any of God's characteristics.

But even if you are neat, disciplined and controlled, the overriding essence is your spirit. Everything you try to accomplish can be enhanced or destroyed by your attitude. Even if the actual words you speak are acceptable, your tone of voice conveys your true heart message. You can slice your husband to shreds at forty paces just by uttering the words "Yes, dear" in *that* tone of voice.

"If anyone thinks himself to be religious, and yet does not bridle his tongue but deceives his own heart, this man's religion is worthless" (James 1:26). Ouch! James always hits right at the heart of the matter. A nagging woman is certainly not one who bridles her tongue. Does Sunday morning sound like this at your house? "Are you gonna go to church with me this morning? Why not? You *never* go with me. If you'd help me get the kids ready for Sunday school, I wouldn't have to rush." Nag, nag, nag! "The contentions of a wife are a constant dripping" (Prov. 19:13).

What man would want to go to church with *that* woman? He probably can't wait for her to leave so he can have some peace and quiet! The old addage, "You can catch more flies with honey . . ." is still true.

"I've been married to one for more than forty years." With iron-gray hair, the woman sitting next to me spoke harshly of her non-Christian husband. She shook her head and turned away from me, the bitterness of her years hung like a heavy odor around her. The "poor me" attitude she displayed unfortunately is typical of many women in her situation.

The spirit we project will permeate and color the very environment around us. How much better the atmosphere would be if we began each day, each conversation, with a smile. It's such a simple thing to do, merely lift the corners of your mouth. With a little practice you can let it spread to light your eyes and eventually warm your voice! But the reward will be the response shown in those who see it.

A smile can soften the harshest words and smooth over many difficult situations. As Christians we have available to us the power of the indwelling Holy Spirit, and I can't imagine the Holy Spirit having the "poor me" attitude or a self-pitying "nag, nag, nag" disposition. Rather, Scripture assures us that "the fruit of the Spirit is love, joy, peace, patience, kindness, goodness, faithfulness, gentleness, self-control; against such things there is no law" (Gal. 5:22-23).

Just think what an abundance of these attributes displayed in our homes would do. The very atmosphere would change. Think about just one of these for a moment: *joy*. Have you ever walked into a room when people were laughing? It isn't long until you are laughing, too, even though you may not know what is so funny. Laughter is contagious! So is joy. People are attracted to a person who is happy, smiles a lot, is calm, peaceful, patient, kind, etc.

As recorded in John 12:32, Jesus said, "And I, if I be lifted up from the earth, will draw all men to Myself." If we display (or lift up) the characteristics of Christ, people will naturally draw closer where they can be exposed to the Spirit of Christ and His message.

The Apostle Paul explained to the Christians at Colossae that this attitude was something they had to choose to use—an action they had to take. "And so, as those who have been chosen by God, holy and beloved, put on a heart of compassion, kindness, humility, gentleness and patience; bearing with one another, and forgiving each other . . . and beyond all these things put on love, which is the perfect bond of unity" (Col. 3:12-14).

The spirit of joy, the perfume of gentleness, the essence of love—who could possibly resist the charm of this kind of wife? Everything we do, everything we say, is constantly a reminder to those living close to us that *this is what it means to be a Christian.* Will we draw them to Christ with a spirit of joy or repulse them with an odor of bitterness? The choice is ours.

1. How can you show the true spirit of joy to your husband today?
2. What would Christ's attitude be about the spirit you are now displaying?
3. What scriptures offer the right example for you to follow?
4. What changes can you make in your personal attitude?
5. If you need to lose some weight, be more disciplined in your home life, or make yourself more attractive in personality or appearance, how do you plan to make those changes?
6. Promise to claim:
   "The joy of the Lord is your strength" (Neh. 8:10).

Chapter 14: *Running Against the Wind*

"Let us also lay aside every encumbrance . . . and let us run with endurance the race that is set before us" (Heb. 12:1).

"But don't I have *any* rights?" Ilene had been studying the third chapter of 1 Peter. Frustrated, she twisted a strand of hair around one finger. "This is the twentieth century—and we live in America. People are supposed to be free. Yet these verses seem to nail wives back into the slavery women have fought so hard to escape.

"If I live the way the Bible says," she said, shaking her head in bewilderment, "it would be denying the blood of our ancestors. It's . . . it's un-American!"

With an understanding smile I filled the empty cup in front of her. "I know how you feel. There was a time when something inside of me screamed for release. Time and again I wondered: When do I get to be *me*?"

We both watched the steam rise from our teacups, twisting and swirling before it dissipated. "It seems we're always under someone's thumb," I continued. "As children we're subject to parents and teachers; then we bow to the wishes of our employers. You'd think at least in marriage we'd have some freedom. But even there the responsibilities of home and family become our master."

"Even the Bible is against us." Ilene fingered the open

pages in front of her. "I think God is asking *too* much this time."

There was a time when I would have agreed with Ilene; but time, experience, and the truth of following the Scriptures have changed my opinion. As I've said before, I'm a very strong-willed person. But then, so is my husband. We've had more than our share of head-butting sessions. I knew my way was best. I'd try so hard to point our family in the right direction spiritually, but it was like running against the wind. I'd end up exhausted, having made little or no progress.

When people have different points of view, it creates friction (1 Tim. 6:3-5), and friction is an encumbrance to running the race Christ has set before us. How can we set aside the friction of opposite views?

The precious mother of Jesus gives us an excellent example to follow. Mary was chosen of God. A unique woman among women, she was selected to bear God's Son. Of *all* women, she could be trusted to rear this divine child. You'd think that with all she was going to do for God, she would have special privileges. She should have the right to live a perfect life with no major problems.

But Mary, far from the placid person we've been programmed to believe, had a tough, tenacious character. At the very outset of her contact with the angel Gabriel she chose to set aside her rights. Voicing no doubts about the kind of life God was asking her to lead, she yielded her right to a normal life. "And Mary said, 'Behold the bondslave of the Lord; be it done to me according to your word' " (Luke 1:38).

This word *bondslave* or *handmaid* is the same word Paul uses in Rom. 1:1 when he describes his relationship to Christ. It means literally "tied to" the master. The position could be either voluntary or involuntary. But once done, the slave had no rights—of *any* kind.

It takes strength of character to yield our rights willingly. Mary had to be strong and courageous. She knew there would be ridicule from her peers to endure. If you were Mary's parents, would you believe the explanation she gave for becoming pregnant outside the finalizing of her marriage vows?

And later, when she saw this same divine Son dying on a cross, we see no condemnation of God from Mary's lips. That's real strength of character!

Being a Christian is not the placid, namby-pamby life the world would have us believe it is. As the writer declares in Heb. 12:1, we are to run with *endurance* the course Christ has chosen for us. Any runner can tell you that it takes strength both in body and in character to run a full race. A runner has to give up—in a commitment sense—any number of "rights." For instance, they give up the right to sit in the stands and comfortably watch the other runners, the right to loll in bed late or eat tons of fattening foods.

The same thing is true when we choose to follow Christ. We need to trim away any rights that would slow us down or cause us to stumble.

"I'm a Christian and therefore I have the right to be happy." I've heard that statement any number of times. But the truth is, we are admonished to be *joyful*. "Let them also that love thy name be joyful in thee" (Ps. 5:11, KJV). Too often we are so caught up in pursuing our own happiness that we lose sight of what true joy is. It is a joy derived from God that is consistent despite our husbands or our family—it cannot be added to nor taken away from by anyone. It is found in running the race that God has for us, not by doing what we want.

In a sense, what Ilene was saying about God asking too much of her was that she couldn't be happy living God's way. She felt that the only thing that would make her happy was to have her own way.

As Christians we are slaves, bound by love, to Christ. In that sense we have already chosen to yield our personal rights to Him. Can a slave insist on having his own way?

All of us place our own values on different things in life. What is important to you may not be important to me. But consider with me some of the rights we can yield to Christ. Could your list include the emotions surrounding your unsaved husband? Are you angry or bitter toward God because your husband isn't a Christian? (Heb. 12:15). Or, what about yielding the right to unlimited Christian activities? Do you feel that God isn't being fair with you?

Sometimes we falsely entertain the idea that God is unjust with us. Since we have given Him our hearts and chosen to follow Christ, shouldn't we now have the right to fill our time with all those delightful things that other Christians do? In reality—the answer is no!

Lillian is always leaving her unsaved husband at home alone. She spends her time having lunch with her Christian friends, attending church social activities or Christian meetings. In themselves, those things aren't wrong. It's just that her husband should come before those activities.

Jesus wants us to yield ourselves to Him so that He can mold us into the best person we can become. It doesn't matter whether we have a Christian husband or not. When we put Christ first we are yielding our rights to Him. His primary word to us is to lovingly serve our husbands.

God has given each of us a unique course to run. Each of us has a different path with personalized obstacles. That's why no one person's life can be the same as another person's. What works for someone else may not work in your case. But in all of us God is trying to develop our inward qualities.

It is God's present plan for me that I become His best by having this unique husband. Many of the difficult circumstances I face are not meant to deter my Christian life but to confirm it and strengthen it. Every time I run into a "brick wall," a situation or circumstance that I can't change, I ask God to change *me*. I'd rather that God would change the circumstances so life would be easier for me. But when He says no, then the only other solution is to change *me* to fit the situation.

I don't know how many times I've found a verse that seemed to say I had the right to demand that God answer my prayer. I'd claim it, storming heaven, insisting that God change my husband. Instead, God very lovingly has changed me. I've learned that I can be more of "me" outside the cloistered walls of my church—because my husband is *there*. If I stand as close to God as I possibly can, then He in turn will use me in my husband's sphere. By yielding my right to spend extra time in the church, God gave it back to me in a better way.

Whenever we yield a "right" to God we make an inner change. This causes us to develop new inward qualities. Jesus, though He was the very Son of God, yielded His rights and chose to do the will of the Father. "Although He was a Son, He learned obedience from the things which He suffered" (Heb. 5:8). Not only did He choose to yield, but the Father deemed it best for Him. "For it was fitting for Him, for whom are all things, and through whom are all things, in bringing many sons to glory, to perfect the author of their salvation through suffering" (Heb. 2:10). This suffering was His training; it was what His Father wanted. Because of it, when the proper time came, He was able to pray, "Not My will, but Thine be done" (Luke 22:42).

There are three major steps in making this change in our lives. The first step is to identify the rights involved. List the things that are bothering you. Then take the second step: transfer ownership of those rights to God. Paul said to the church at Galatia, "I have been crucified with Christ; and it is no longer I who live, but Christ lives in me"

(Gal. 2:20). Nail your list of *I want* items to the cross of Christ. Again Paul said, "But may it never be that I should boast, except in the cross of our Lord Jesus Christ, through which the world has been crucified to me, and I to the world" (Gal. 6:14).

This isn't a unique thought. Paul challenged the church at Ephesus to "lay aside the old self . . . and put on the new self. . ." (Eph. 4:22-24).

But the process won't be complete without the third step: praise God for the results. Job, in his extremity, cried out, "The Lord gave and the Lord has taken away. Blessed be the name of the Lord" (Job 1:21). Praise is a vital part of our Christian walk. We can't be complete without it. Philippians 4:4 says, "Rejoice in the Lord always; again I will say, rejoice!"

Although we each have a separate race to run, the goal is the same for all of us. And the only way we can reach that goal is to keep our eyes fixed on Christ.

He has promised to be with us, to help us, to guide us. How then can we give up the race and just walk away? It *is* true that when we yield our rights we will be tested. But that testing should be welcome because it will prove the power of God and the quality of our servanthood. He can be trusted to give back to us in pure form the essence of whatever we yield to Him. Then we can join in giving Him praise.

1. If you have been clinging tightly to the "right" to have a Christian husband, will you consider yielding this to Christ?
2. What would Christ's attitude be regarding your "rights"?
3. What scripture offers the best example to follow?
4. What personal attitude should you adopt?
5. What action do you need to take to put into effect the

yielding of your rights to the purifying power of God?
6. Promise to claim:
   "The things you have learned and received and heard
   and seen in me, practice these things; and the God of
   peace shall be with you" (Phil. 4:9).

Chapter 15: *Romance—The Spice of Life*

"You have made my heart beat faster with a single glance of your eyes" (Song of Sol. 4:9).

"I can't believe this is happening!" Nancy's eyes sparkled as she informed me, "This is the third time my husband has sent me flowers recently." She proudly displayed the beautiful roses in their vase.

"Mmm, they're gorgeous!" I sniffed appreciatively. "Let me see the card." Playfully I reached toward the attached note.

"Not on your life!" She snatched it out of my reach, blushing. "It's—well—it's *personal*."

I raised a knowing eyebrow, enjoying her gentle embarrassment. She laughed at my action. It was a moment of triumph for both of us.

Less than a year before, Nancy's love life had been nothing to blush about. In fact, it was a major source of contention in her marriage. At that time she had confided, "It never fails—whenever I plan to go to choir practice, Bible class or church, that's the moment Marty wants to be intimate. It always ends in a fight, and I either leave the house angry or give in and go to bed with him—still angry!"

We had spent months searching the Scriptures for God's guidance on Nancy's negative attitude toward sex. We had prayed together and brainstormed ideas to improve her situation. Now, the roses in front of us were eloquent testimony to the change in Nancy—and the consequent change in Marty.

Roses say, "I love you," touching the romantic heartstrings of a woman in a way that little else can. Of course, romance is only one expression of love. Many strong marriages survive intact without much romance—"nice but not necessary."

What *is* romance, anyway? A teenage girl growing up on a literary diet of heart-and-flowers "romances" no doubt thinks it is synonymous with love. Her youthful idealism is rather engaging and will sometimes last clear through courtship, wedding and the honeymoon! But the flowers and candy, whispered endearments and tender embraces are only *expressions* of love—that deep commitment to one another which says "we belong to each other" no matter what!

The area Nancy had to work on in order to change her attitude toward sex involved the concept of commitment. When she realized that Marty actually was asking, "Do you *really* love me?" and that loving him meant wanting the very best for him, she was able to view their intimacy in a new way. And she also came to realize that romance in marriage is a two-way street—that she shouldn't merely sit back and wait to be wooed.

Perhaps one of the best love stories in the Bible is found in the Book of Ruth. Picture a young widow living with her aged mother-in-law in a foreign country. Add the poignancy of being childless and poor. Ruth had to scrounge the bits of grain dropped in the fields or they would starve.

It's a perfect setting for a true romance. When Boaz first saw Ruth in his field, he just had to find out who she was (Ruth 2:5). Immediately he started protecting her, providing security, extra grain and even water. Later, he called her to his table and shared his food.

I wonder if there were stars in her eyes when she went home that night. Surely she must have dreamed about the man who had so gallantly swept into her life.

But Ruth's love story has a couple of twists in its plot. She is a loving, obedient girl who willingly subjects herself to her mother-in-law's directions. In typical female fashion, she bathes, pampers and primps herself, and puts on her best clothes (Ruth 3:3). Then she takes some personal risks. I wonder how fast her heart beat as she waited for Boaz to finally lie down that night. Did she hold her breath as she tiptoed to his threshing-floor bed and ever so carefully curled up at his feet?

These customs seem strange to us, but were within the confines of Jewish tradition. She was appealing in private to Boaz on the basis of her desire to have Naomi's land redeemed by a rightful kinsman and by her desire that Boaz exercise his right as the one to marry her (Deut. 25:5-10). She would not have appealed to the latter had she not sensed that Boaz felt the same. But the final choice was left to Boaz: by going to him under the cover of darkness, he was free from social pressure to act.

In true heroic manner Boaz not only accepts her, but is both discreet and cunning in securing Ruth's hand in marriage (Ruth 3 and 4).

Ruth's love was unconditional. Not self-centered or self-seeking, she did not publicly demand that Boaz court her or follow the customs of her own country. She was willing to take the first step and be the one to take the risk. But the results were well worth it. Not only did he marry her, making her the mistress of a wealthy household, but she became one of the "chosen" ones to be included in the direct line to Christ (Matt. 1:5).

We sigh, put the book down and walk away with the gentle warmth of another love story. But does it need to end there? What about your life? What about my life?

Does your "hero" come home from work, plop down in front of the TV, or hide behind the newspaper until he falls asleep? Okay, so he isn't Prince Charming anymore. What are *you* going to do about it?

Of all the chapters in this book, I shied away from writing this one. I guess it's because it took me so long to learn the place of romance and sex in a marriage. I'd been raised, like many of my Christian contemporaries, to never, *never* talk about sex! It was a necessary part of marriage, but nice Christian girls simply did not discuss it. Unfortunately, that attitude so strongly colored my thinking that it took me years to tear down this barrier to a happier union. Nice girls didn't "burn with passion" and Christian women must never be seductive!

So *what* are nice girls like Ruth and Esther doing putting on perfume and their most attractive clothing? They were not afraid to be as appealing as possible. Perhaps some of us need to take the bedroom "out of the closet"! Since the Creator is the one who invented marriage and sex, maybe it *is* all right to talk about it!

I'm afraid the non-Christian husband will view his Christian wife's sex hangups as very prudish. With this strained background and conflict of values, it's no wonder some bedroom scenes are less than satisfying. When his secretary shows up at the office picnic in something less than a bikini, the contrast with our own carefully modest attire is considerable; how can the Christian wife compete with that? She can compete in private!

It's essential to learn this one incredible lesson: it's all right for a Christian to enjoy sex! In fact, for the spiritually single woman, this one facet of marriage is the place where we can best show God's love. "For this cause a man shall leave his father and mother, and shall cleave to his wife; and the two shall become one flesh" (Eph. 5:31).

How can we change from the restricted view of sex we've been raised with to being an enchanting, entrancing and even seductive wife? The place to begin is with our attitude. If I truly love my husband and want the very best for him, I will want to please him in every way I possibly can. And my being sexually appealing surely will please him!

If you are not quite sure how to go about this, take a cue from Sara Anne. "I've noticed," she shared one afternoon, "that right after I've seen a romantic movie I enjoy making love to my husband more than usual."

"The same thing sometimes happens for me when I read a romantic story." My own experiences suddenly clicked into place. If my basic attitude is right, these kinds of romances can create an emotional setting and give ideas for being romantic to your husband.

On a very practical level, we need to raise our level of sensual awareness to make this transition easier. For example, invest in a sexy nightgown—not only one that pleases your husband, but something that makes you feel very special. (I hope you're not sleeping in your husband's old undershirts! Not only is such attire unsightly, it shows how you view yourself.)

The sense of touch is useful, too. Touch your husband— often. Run your fingers through his hair or lightly across the back of his neck. Slip your arm through his when you are walking together. Instead of sitting across from him at a restaurant, sit next to him where you can feel his body brush yours. It's pleasing for both of you.

You could even think about buying some satin sheets! And, for yourself, (and for him!), some delightfully feminine undergarments. Many of the newer fabrics are sensuous to touch.

Try teasing your husband or making sexy innuendos. It may take practice, but it will really add some spice to your life—and to his.

If your husband can't seem to bring himself to respond to you with romance of his own, don't give up! Give of yourself unselfishly without expecting your love to be returned in the same way—that's the way God loves us! In the long run, this will be a far stronger testimony to your husband than anything you can say in words.

As I indicated earlier, one of the first changes Nancy made was to stop fighting Marty when he chose an inopportune time to be intimate. She decided to put him first, even if it meant being late to church. It only took a few times before Marty realized that Nancy was taking time to meet his needs. In reaction, he began to choose a better time for their lovemaking and Nancy was free to attend church on time.

Making these changes isn't always easy, but no one said you had to do it alone. Ask God to help you fulfill the sensual side of marriage. Are you feeling a little crabby or out-of-sorts? Ask God to help you respond to your husband. "And whatever we ask we receive from Him, because we keep His commandments and do the things that are pleasing in His sight" (1 John 3:22).

Marriage, particularly the marriage bed, is the most intimate object lesson we have of the Christian's union with God. "For your husband is your Maker, whose name is the Lord of hosts" (Isa. 54:5). In the fifth chapter of Ephesians Paul makes this same analogy. "For the husband is the head of the wife, as Christ also is the head of the church. He himself being the Savior of the body. But as the church is subject to Christ, so also the wives ought to be to their husbands in everything" (Eph. 5:23-24).

Paul goes on to remind us that husbands and wives become one flesh and then adds this clarification: "This mystery is great; but I am speaking with reference to Christ and the church" (Eph. 5:32).

If we can change our view of the marriage bed from one of duty to one of beauty, we can unite in love with our husband in the same delightful way Christ unites with the church.

1. Exactly how can you show Christ's love to your husband in this particular situation?
2. What would Christ's attitude be?
3. What scripture offers the right example to follow?
4. What personal attitude should you adopt?
5. What action do you need to take?
6. Promise to claim:
   "In all thy ways acknowledge him, and he shall direct thy paths" (Prov. 3:6, KJV).

Chapter 16: *When Bad Gets Worse*

"Fear not, for I am with you. Do not be dismayed. I am your God. I will strengthen you; I will help you; I will uphold you with my victorious right hand" (Isa. 41:10, TLB).

She knocked on my door late one night. Her face bruised and swollen, she pled, "Mrs. Mitchell, may I please come in?"

Her story of abuse, although shocking, is unfortunately more common than we care to admit. It wasn't the first time this had occurred and, unless something changed, I knew it wouldn't be the last.

"Why does God let this happen to me?" Her words pierced my heart. After an evening at the tavern her husband had come home and vented his anger on this lovely wife before stumbling off to bed.

There were two precious children sleeping in that same house, and I knew the time had come for her to face some hard realities. Her greatest responsibility was to protect those children, but she didn't have the strength to do it alone.

Although the attitude changes and personal improvements we've been talking about are often the answer in troubled relationships, sometimes they are only a Band-Aid on a blood-gushing wound. When we have done everything there is to do and we still find ourselves in an impossible situation, what then?

Does God expect us to remain in an abusive situation? There may be some people reading this chapter who may not agree with its contents or may not understand this situation. If so, I ask you to read with a compassionate heart. There are women in some very trying circumstances who are hurting twenty-four hours of every day and many do not have the strength or knowledge to help themselves.

If any of us saw an animal being brutally beaten or starved, we would quickly call the authorities. But how strange that if the same situation involves people, we try to place the blame on the victim! We are so quick to judge— "She must really be a shrew to drive her husband to drink like that!" Shouldn't we be even quicker to effect a rescue?

There are evil people in this world and we suffer because of them. In the Scriptures we find many examples of atrocities: Herodias, who requested (and received) the head of John the Baptist (Matt. 14:1-11); King Herod, who slew all those precious, innocent babies (Matt. 2:16); the Egyptian Pharaoh (Ex. 1); and many more.

Sometimes God in His love and mercy provided a time and means of escape. For example, through Moses He delivered the Israelites from their oppressors. And for His own Son, God sent an angel with a message telling Mary and Joseph to escape into a safe land.

When the time comes, it may be necessary for the Christian wife to physically remove herself for her own protection and for the protection of her children. Abuse simply cannot be tolerated!

If you are in an abusive situation where either you or your children are battered or sexually assaulted, my heart cries out to you. In all the love that is within me, I beg of you to seek the help you so desperately need. Quit hiding behind the cobweb wall of excuses—they offer you no protection and most often others can see right through them. You can't wait any longer.

This is the time to act. There are any number of agencies waiting to help you. In the case of physical abuse, call the police—*now*! They will help you find a place to live and direct you to people who will offer all the assistance you need. In many states there are women's shelters just for battered and abused wives.

The Department of Social and Health Services has a Child Protection Division. These people know exactly what to do to help you. No excuse can ever be great enough when you must stand at the edge of your child's grave. Believe me, it can happen to you. Call someone right now.

There are others who will help you, too. Any physician or clergyman can contact the right people in your locality—but please, be honest with them. Tell them the truth no matter how much it shatters your pride. And remember, it won't be easy; but if you have the "guts" to take his beatings, you can surely pick up the telephone. One woman told me much later, "My only regret is that I didn't leave sooner."

Perhaps your situation isn't quite this extreme. Yet it is beyond all the self-help suggestions that have been made. Please *do consider* seeking professional counseling. Many pastors today have excellent counseling skills, or at least they can direct you to someone who does. God has offered us so many promises of His help, but we must *ask* for it (Matt. 7:7-11). The same thing is true for human help—you must ask.

What if it's too late for counseling? Or, counseling doesn't work and your husband chooses to leave you? Let me offer you some points to consider.

The first one is that you probably are feeling rejected. Crushed by the realization that you have been cast aside, you may be wallowing in self-pity. Or, you may be hiding at home feeling that you have no value. Unable to face all the realities, you may be caught in the whirlpool of "what if's." "What if I had done *this*?" or "What if I had changed *that*?" Or possibly you are hoping he'll come back to you.

All I can say here is—you can't go back. You cannot change the past, so it's better to get on with today. The future will take care of itself. Drowning in self-pity certainly doesn't bring any glory to God.

But the Scripture does offer us some consolation. Inside the cover of my Bible is a slip of paper with the following four verses. It's a constant reminder of God's comfort when I am in difficult or trying circumstances:

2 Cor. 1:4-6	God comforts us that we may comfort others.
2 Cor. 2:14	Christ's triumph in us is seen by others.
2 Cor. 4:16-18	These little troubles are winning permanent reward out of all proportion to pain.
2 Cor. 12:9	"My grace is sufficient"—weakness offers a deeper experience of the power of Christ.

Whenever I feel completely overwhelmed by the chaos around me, I read these passages, and one of them usually starts me on the road to recovery.

I think it's important for us to remember that no matter how difficult things are, we are not alone. God has promised to be with us: He has not rejected us. And, there is always someone else who is going through similar circumstances and they need comforting, too.

"Comfort, oh, comfort my people, says your God. Speak tenderly to Jerusalem and tell her that her sad days are gone. Her sins are pardoned, and the Lord will give her twice as many blessings as he gave her punishment before" (Isa. 40:1, 2, TLB). You see, the Lord wants us to let go of the past and accept His calm and peace. By reaching out to others who are hurting, we begin the healing process within ourselves.

God wants us to let go of the shock of disbelief ("This can't be happening to me," or, "I'll pretend that he'll be back home soon"), the stabbing anger (at *him*, at God, perhaps at yourself), the heavy burden of guilt (it's all my fault), and the blackness of depression (if this is life, I don't want to live). Instead, God offers us His peace, His release, His comfort. All this can be ours when we come to an acceptance of the reality of our situation and seek God's help.

In this chapter we have faced the big question, "How bad is *bad*? Only you can answer it. What is intolerable for one person may not be for another. But as you carefully, prayerfully review your life, be honest with yourself and God. Let Him comfort and guide you.

1. In your current situation, to whom do you need to reach out and express God's love?
2. What would Christ's attitude be if He lived in your home?
3. What verses in Scripture can be your guidelines?
4. Letting go of the past, what should your personal attitude be?
5. If you have seen yourself in this chapter, what steps do you plan to take today? Do you need to call the police? A clergyman? A counselor? Or, that person you know who is hurting as much as you are?
6. Promise to claim:
   "When you go through deep waters and great trouble, I will be with you. When you go through rivers of difficulty, you will not drown! When you walk through the fire of oppression, you will not be burned up—the flames will not consume you" (Isa. 43:2, TLB).

Chapter 17: *Small Beginnings*

"Do not despise this small beginning, for the eyes of the
Lord rejoice to see the work begin" (Zech. 4:10, TLB).

I cannot finish this book without including the promise
of small beginnings. In Chapter 15 we saw some changes
taking place. Nancy's husband sent her flowers and eventually changed a pattern that allowed her to attend church on
time. Back in Chapter 3, Darlene saw a small change in
Tom. As she relaxed in his circle of friends, his bitterness
melted. Their life together had a chance to grow when the
bitterness was gone.

Cathy, in Chapter 4, experienced a small beginning in
her husband's attitude. When she took the time to obtain
his permission to take the children to church, George no
longer harassed her.

So often we are only watching for the big things. Yet it's
the small things that show the first signs of change. In the
valley where we live, throughout the winter we periodically
experience Chinook winds. These are sudden warm winds
that slurp up the snow and ice, bringing a tremendous temperature change. In a matter of hours we can go from sub-
freezing to spring-like conditions. It's always in the back of
our minds: "Will we get a Chinook today?" Whenever we go
outside we glance toward the Blue Mountains for some sign
that will provide hope for a release from winter.

It begins at the very tips of the snow-covered mountain peaks. A tiny hint of blue color slowly creeps downward. Long before the winds brush our chapped faces and we start shedding that extra sweater, the news has spread. "It's a Chinook!" It may still be nippy outside, but everywhere there's a sparkle in people's eyes and a lilt to their step that reflects the good news of hope.

Small beginnings are like that. Just a hint, just a promise of better days ahead. We need to sharpen our focus so we don't miss these early signs.

In Chapter 15 we talked about Ruth's story. She had some of the best hints I've seen. Watch the progression. At first Boaz said, "Stay here with my maids" (Ruth 2:8). He didn't want her to leave. That showed a sliver of interest. Then in verse 9 he adds, "When you are thirsty, go to the water jars and drink." This showed more than just a passive attitude. He cared about her physical safety and whether or not she was thirsty. I can just see the knowing looks that passed quickly from servant to servant as they noted their master's interest in this stranger.

When Ruth herself questions his motives, Boaz comes back with an excuse that sounds no different than a love-struck teenager. "Well . . . uh . . . you see, I've heard about you . . . and, uh . . . you need some help . . . and . . . may God bless you" (*my* paraphrase of verses 11 and 12). But by lunchtime Ruth is beginning to get a clearer picture when Boaz asks her to eat at his table (v. 14).

When taken alone, none of these incidents seem like much. But with an eye of hope we can put them together step by step to see the signs of change.

Samuel, too, experienced a small beginning. His dream was for a godly man to be king over Israel (1 Sam. 16:1). He was still grieving over Saul when God handed him the first hint of hope. He was sent to the household of Jesse to anoint the next king. Instead of finding a full-grown man ready to assume the kingship, Samuel is told to anoint a *child*! "There remains yet the youngest, and behold, he is tending the sheep" (1 Sam. 16:11). But God had told Samuel to look not for the big things but for the small ones. "God sees not as man sees, for man looks at the outward appearance, but the Lord looks at the heart" (1 Sam. 16:7). It was this child who would one day be the godly king Samuel longed to see.

For David it was a small beginning, too. All he had was the secret knowledge that he had been anointed—chosen to be a future king. I wonder what he thought as he went back out to the fields to tend the sheep. "Was this a proper place for a future king? Would it really come true?"

When I first attended a Bible Study Fellowship class, I was struck by the story of its beginning. Miss Johnson, a missionary, was approached by five women asking her to lead them in a Bible study. She agreed, but told them she wouldn't "spoon-feed" them. Insisting that they follow her step-by-step presentation involving individual study, the embryo of Bible Study Fellowship was formed. Since then, more than 100,000 men and women in six countries have followed those same steps to a deeper, personal knowledge of the Bible.

What if she had said no, or couldn't be bothered with only five women? One result would have been a lack in my own spiritual life. It was a Bible Study Fellowship class that started my personal quest for a new knowledge of God.

As Christian women, what small beginnings can we look for in our unequally yoked marriages? Start by watching for an attitude change. Has your husband backed off in intensity of opposition? Has he shifted a normal pattern to one that makes life better for you?

Take note of any improved change of attitude and praise God for it. Paul was talking to the Thessalonians when he said, "In everything give thanks; for this is God's will for you in Christ Jesus" (1 Thess. 5:18). Praise is the salt of our prayers, the catalyst that unites our request with God's answers.

Paul also admonished the Ephesians to be "speaking to one another in psalms and hymns and spiritual songs, singing and making melody with your heart to the Lord; always giving thanks for all things in the name of our Lord Jesus Christ to God, even the Father" (Eph. 5:19, 20).

With our praise we can have the security of all the promises in the Bible. I haven't begun to list all the ones that apply to us as spiritually single women. We are told to test God, to prove His power in our lives. He has promised blessing after blessing.

"I the Lord, am your God, who brought you up from the land of Egypt; open your mouth wide and I will fill it" (Ps. 81:10). If you test Him, He will never let you down. "Faithful is He who calls you, and He also will bring it to pass" (1 Thess. 5:24). But we can't receive these promises unless we step out in faith and try them. It doesn't matter if we think we are too weak, God promises to help us anyway. "He gives strength to the weary, and to him who lacks might He increases power" (Isa. 40:29).

So you see, there is no excuse for us to sit back and cry about our plight in life. God has challenged us, "O taste and see that the Lord is good" (Ps. 34:8, KJV). In every way I've tried to show you that you can't change your husband. That's God's job. But you *can change yourself*—if you want to.

With the Apostle Paul I would "urge you therefore, brethren, by the mercies of God, to present your bodies a living and holy sacrifice, acceptable to God, which is your spiritual service of worship. And do not be conformed to this world, but be transformed by the renewing of your mind, that you may prove what the will of God is, that which is good and acceptable and perfect" (Rom. 12:1, 2).

We have to be willing to yield our whole person to Christ

and be changed. Sometimes I resist when God shows me an area that needs correcting. In those cases I often have to pray, "Lord, make me willing *to be made willing* to change." If in all honesty we are doing everything we know to do, God will honor our efforts. "Those who hopefully wait for Me will not be put to shame" (Isa. 49:23).

Perhaps one of the greatest blessings we will receive from claiming these promises is the resultant peace. In Phil. 4:7 we read, "The peace of God, which surpasses all comprehension, shall guard your hearts and your minds in Christ Jesus." As you make some necessary changes, searching the Scriptures for God's guidance, His peace will fill your heart. You will notice a new, more relaxed atmosphere in your home and a greater contentment in your life.

As the relationships improved in my own home, my husband and I were occasionally able to talk over our views of God, Christ, salvation and Christianity without the fear that the other person would either retreat or attack. In fact, one of the best discussions we had about salvation came as I was writing this manuscript. God allowed me a beautiful glimpse into my husband's soul.

"I do not consider myself an unbeliever," my husband said after reading this book. It was then that I began to look at his point of view.

Somehow I had expected him to walk through the door and announce, "I'm a Christian now." And then he would be instantly mature, fully grown in the Lord and we would never have problems again. Instead, with those simple words, I listened with God's heart as he told me his view of what a believer is. I could see the tiniest beginning of a life in Christ.

How careful I would have to be that in my "right-ness" I wouldn't stamp on his faint spark. God himself promised that He would never extinguish a dimly burning wick or a smoking flax (Isa. 42:3).

It was a beginning—a small one—but it's given me a great deal of hope and peace.

1. What small beginning in your husband's life can you praise God for?
2. What would Christ's attitude be in your current situation?
3. What scripture can you use as an example to follow either in praise or claiming God's peace?
4. What should your personal attitude be?
5. What do you plan to change in your own life as you look at these new small beginnings?
6. Promise to claim:
   "Delight yourself in the Lord; and He will give you the desires of your heart. Commit your way to the Lord, trust also in Him, and He will do it" (Ps. 37:4, 5).